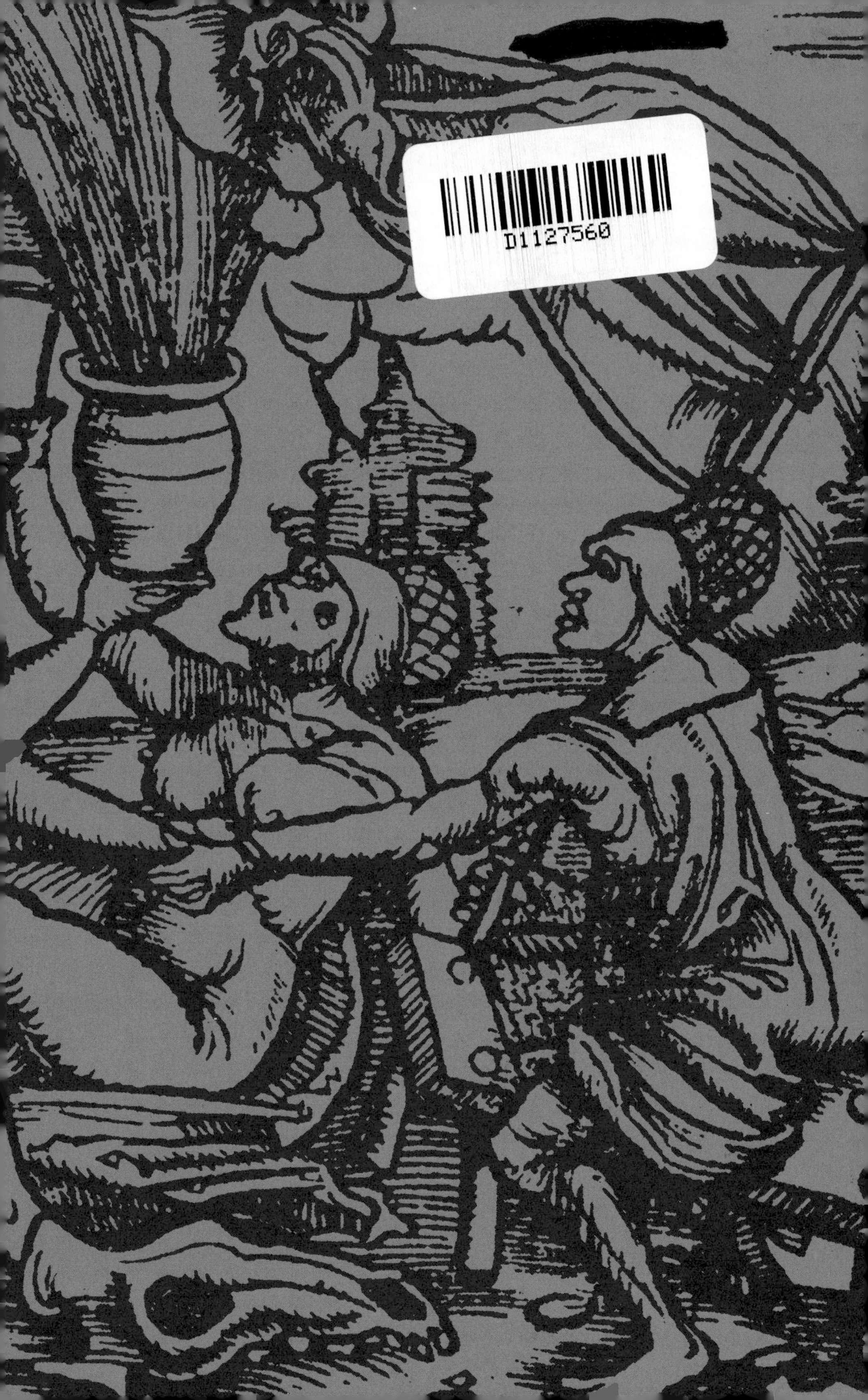

The Dark Horse Book of
Witchcraft

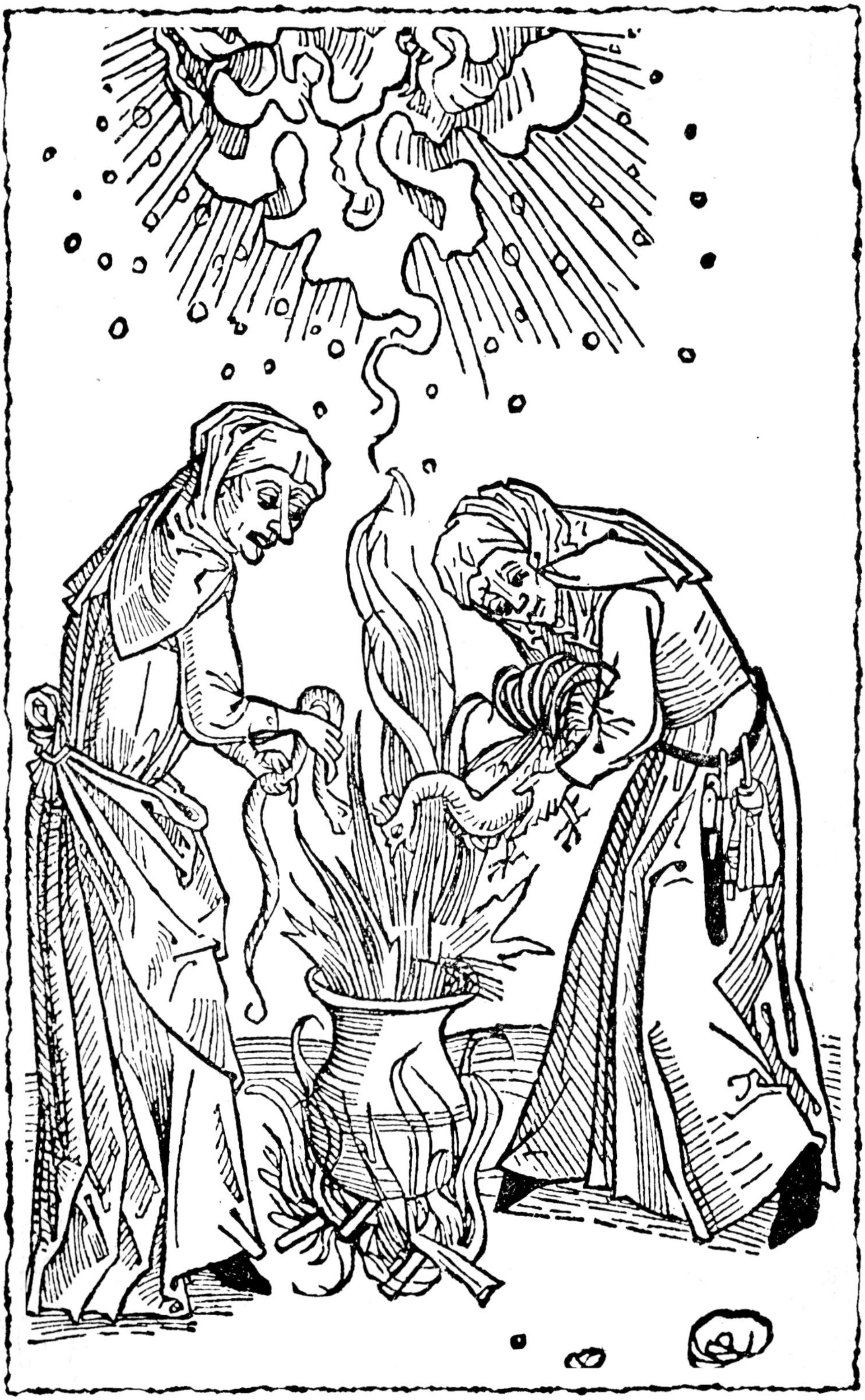

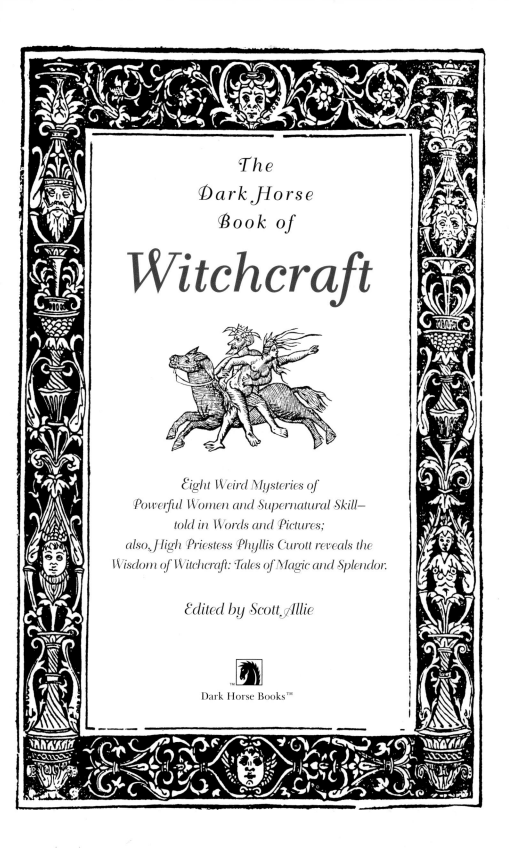

The
Dark Horse
Book of

Witchcraft

Eight Weird Mysteries of
Powerful Women and Supernatural Skill—
told in Words and Pictures;
also, High Priestess Phyllis Curott reveals the
Wisdom of Witchcraft: Tales of Magic and Splendor.

Edited by Scott Allie

Dark Horse Books™

Cover Illustration
Gary Gianni

Cover Design and Colors
Jim Keegan

Assistant Editor
Matt Dryer

Designer
Lani Schreibstein

Art Director
Lia Ribacchi

Publisher
Mike Richardson

Special thanks to
Shawna Ervin-Gore, Jason Hvam, Mark Cox, Dave Land, and to Joshua Bilmes and CASiana Literary Enterprises for the rights to "Mother of Toads."

[redacted]

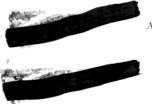

Published by Dark Horse Books
A division of Dark Horse Comics, Inc.
10956 SE Main Street
Milwaukie, OR 97222

[redacted]

First edition
June 2004
ISBN: 1-59307-108-6

[redacted]

1 3 5 7 9 10 8 6 4 2
Printed in China

[redacted]

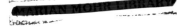

Table of Contents

*In memory of those women and men hanged,
crushed, and left to die in prison, in the summer
and fall of 1692, in Salem, Massachusetts, then the
most advanced port city in the New World.*

Bridget Bishop
George Burroughs
Martha Carrier
Giles Corey
Martha Corey
Lyndia Dustin
Mary Easty
Ann Foster
Sarah Good
Elizabeth Howe
George Jacobs, Sr.
Susannah Martin
Rebecca Nurse
Sarah Osborne
Alice Parker
Mary Parker
John Proctor
Ann Pudeator
Wilmott Reed
Margaret Scott
Roger Toothaker
Samuel Wardwell
Sarah Wilds
John Willard

*Sources conflict on additional casualties, and on
spelling of names.*

Introduction

From earliest childhood, the idea of Witches has given me a rush. I remember running away from the television set, afraid for my life, the first time I saw Margaret Hamilton in green-face in *The Wizard of Oz*. My terror was real—it's one of my earliest memories, one of my most visceral. That Witch roamed my dreams for years afterward. A particularly surreal dream involved a marionette Witch attacking a marionette Dorothy on the eave beneath my windowsill in my grandparents' house. I spent the first part of the next day convinced their battle had actually happened, before realizing it must have been a dream. This sort of thing happens to me all the time.

The most famous real-life Witches in America were not Witches at all, and like Jack the Ripper's victims, their names are less known than their fates. As a kid growing up in Ipswich, Massachusetts, I was fascinated with the history of nearby Salem. Some of the so-called Salem Witches of 1692 were Ipswich residents; some of them, when they were imprisoned, were kept in the Ipswich jail. I worked in the old town library when I was a teenager, and did some research into the Witch history. I wondered if my ancestors on my mother's side, one of the town's founding families, had a role in any of this. At twelve, already interested in the occult, I had sympathy for the victims of the Witch hysteria, whose deaths I found unjust even if I believed they were actually Witches. Imagine my horror when I discovered my one connection to that history in the form of a receipt from one Robert Lord, my ancestor, a blacksmith, for fitting the shackles on the arms and legs of three of the accused women.

This book, like *The Dark Horse Book of Hauntings*, is inspired by the old stories, the old strange fiction of *Weird Tales* and Nathaniel Hawthorne and Lord Dunsany, the depictions of women far more mysterious than what you find in *Charmed* or *Bewitched*. Thanks to Jim Keegan, we're including genuine *Weird Tales* author, Clark Ashton Smith. Returning are contributors from *Hauntings*—Gianni, Mignola (who once again helped me pick the theme for this volume),

Evan Dorkin and Jill Thompson, and Brian Horton, Paul Lee, and Dave Stewart—all of whom I'm grateful to have back, as I'm happy to welcome the new guys. This volume provided me a great opportunity to dig deeper into a different kind of story, the real history of Witchcraft as traced through the works of Charles Godfrey Leland, one of America's greatest and first anthropologists and folklorists. Thanks to Alan Moore, and his exhaustive knowledge of occult history, for helping me prep for the interview, and thanks to Phyllis Curott for the interview, only half of which fit in the space provided here. As a practicing Witch with a background in law and ethics, Phyllis's life work, it could be said, is to shatter the image of the snaggle-toothed old Witch that terrorized me as a child, and that Gary Gianni captured so classically on our cover.

As with *Hauntings*, I suggest reading this book front-to-back, rather than picking out your favorite talent first—or last, if you're one of them disciplined types. Shakespeare and Tony Millionaire conjure up an image that proceeds to change through the course of the book, favoring the villainous (or at least horrible) old crone. The interview, as well as Scott Morse's story, provides the reader with a doorway into the world of the modern Witch, breaking the shackles in which that ancestor of mine helped to bind innocent women.

Abracadabra,

Scott Allie

Portland, Oregon

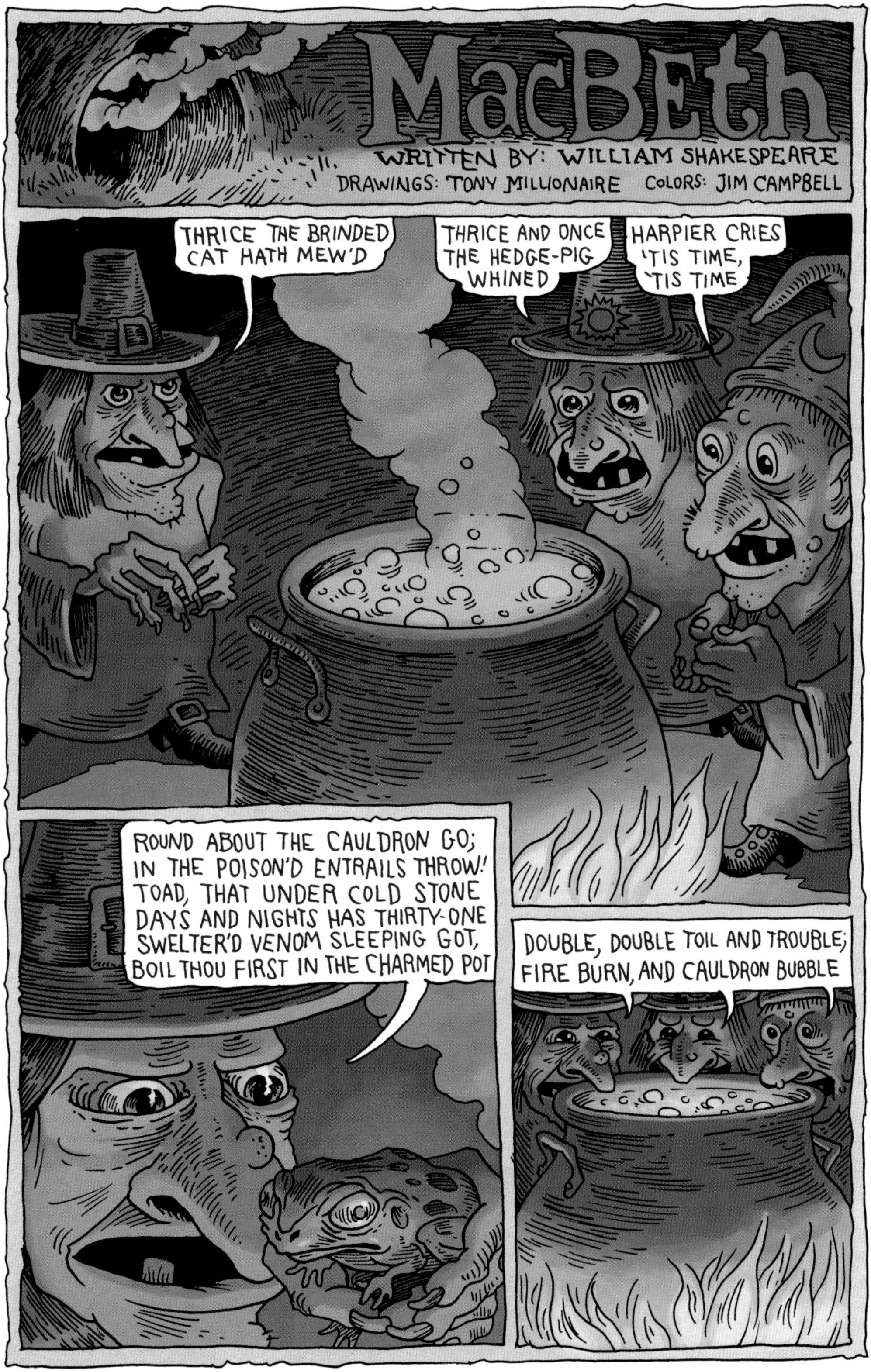
MacBeth
WRITTEN BY: WILLIAM SHAKESPEARE
DRAWINGS: TONY MILLIONAIRE COLORS: JIM CAMPBELL
THRICE THE BRINDED CAT HATH MEW'D
THRICE AND ONCE THE HEDGE-PIG WHINED
HARPIER CRIES 'TIS TIME, 'TIS TIME
ROUND ABOUT THE CAULDRON GO; IN THE POISON'D ENTRAILS THROW! TOAD, THAT UNDER COLD STONE DAYS AND NIGHTS HAS THIRTY-ONE SWELTER'D VENOM SLEEPING GOT, BOIL THOU FIRST IN THE CHARMED POT
DOUBLE, DOUBLE TOIL AND TROUBLE; FIRE BURN, AND CAULDRON BUBBLE

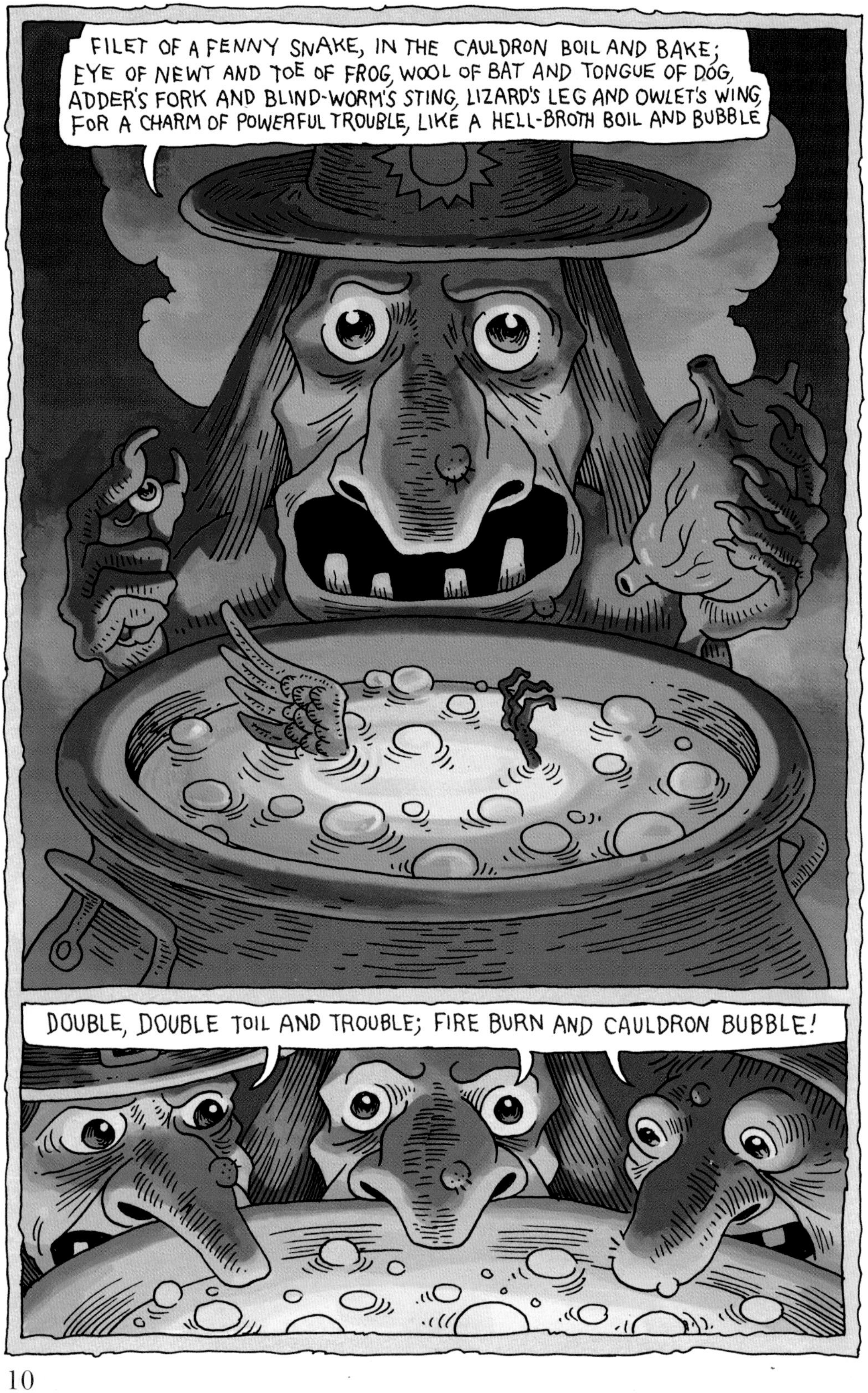
FILET OF A FENNY SNAKE, IN THE CAULDRON BOIL AND BAKE; EYE OF NEWT AND TOE OF FROG, WOOL OF BAT AND TONGUE OF DOG, ADDER'S FORK AND BLIND-WORM'S STING, LIZARD'S LEG AND OWLET'S WING, FOR A CHARM OF POWERFUL TROUBLE, LIKE A HELL-BROTH BOIL AND BUBBLE
DOUBLE, DOUBLE TOIL AND TROUBLE; FIRE BURN AND CAULDRON BUBBLE!

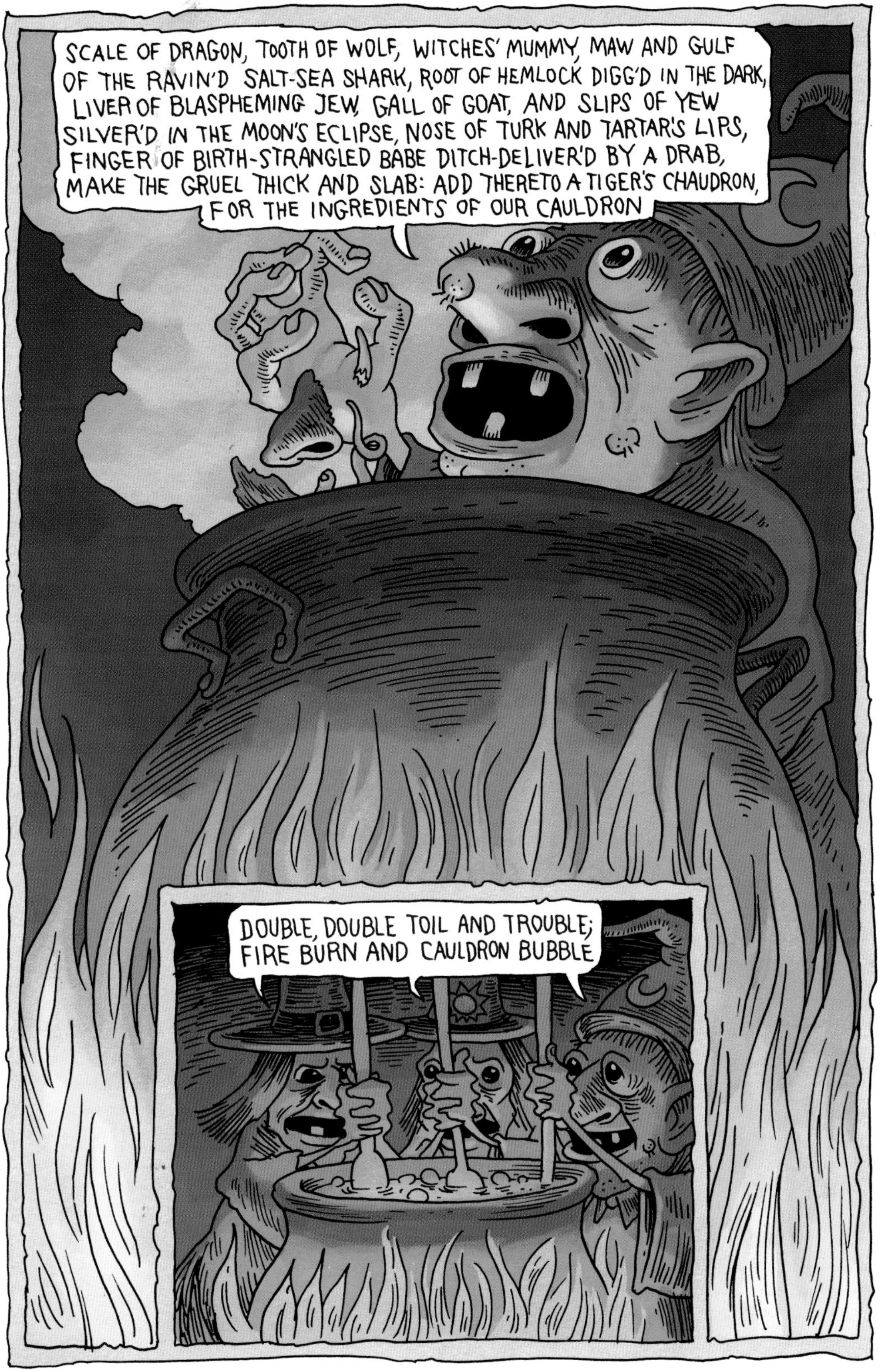
SCALE OF DRAGON, TOOTH OF WOLF, WITCHES' MUMMY, MAW AND GULF OF THE RAVIN'D SALT-SEA SHARK, ROOT OF HEMLOCK DIGG'D IN THE DARK, LIVER OF BLASPHEMING JEW, GALL OF GOAT, AND SLIPS OF YEW SILVER'D IN THE MOON'S ECLIPSE, NOSE OF TURK AND TARTAR'S LIPS, FINGER OF BIRTH-STRANGLED BABE DITCH-DELIVER'D BY A DRAB, MAKE THE GRUEL THICK AND SLAB: ADD THERETO A TIGER'S CHAUDRON, FOR THE INGREDIENTS OF OUR CAULDRON
DOUBLE, DOUBLE TOIL AND TROUBLE; FIRE BURN AND CAULDRON BUBBLE

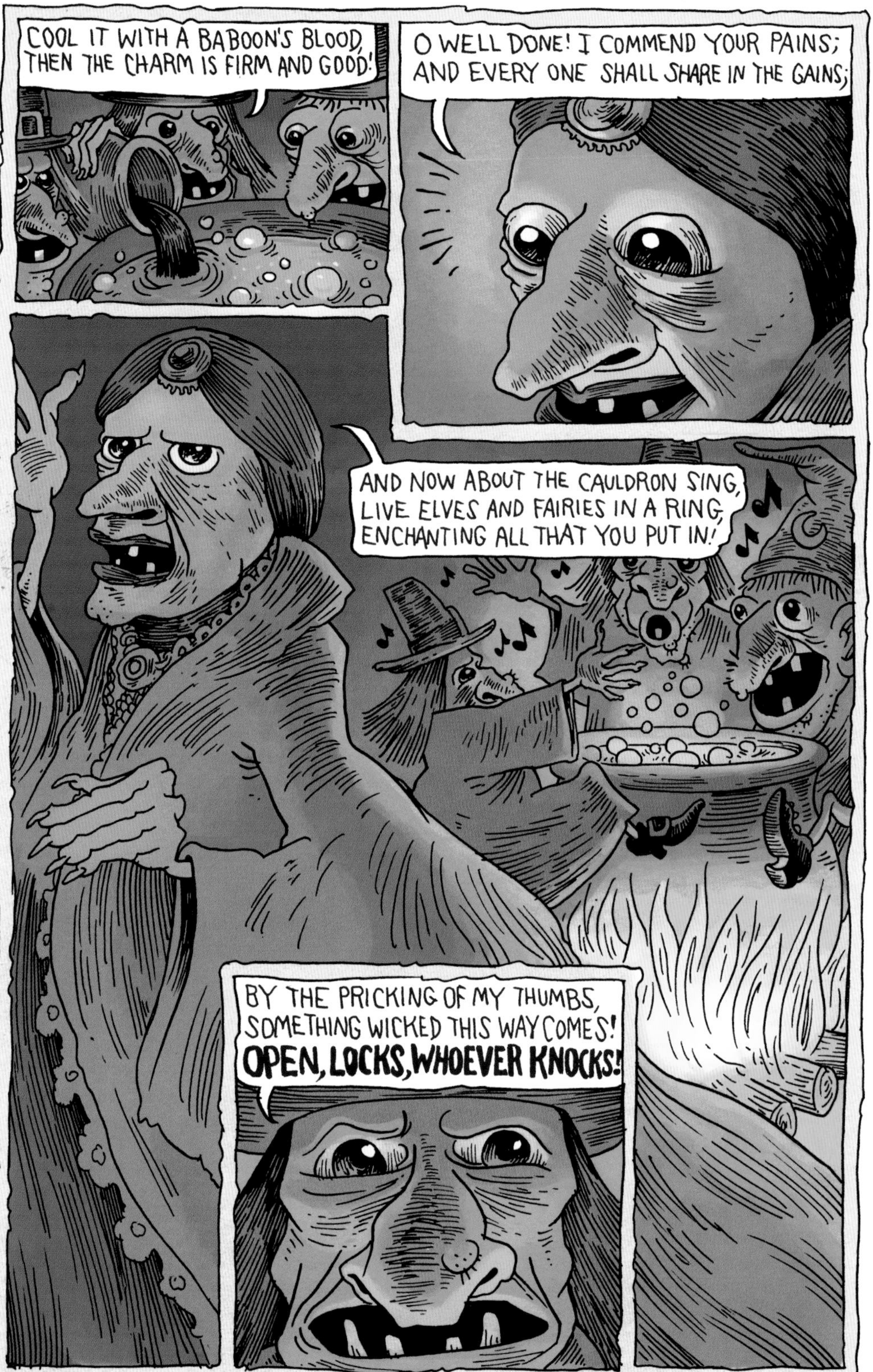
COOL IT WITH A BABOON'S BLOOD, THEN THE CHARM IS FIRM AND GOOD!
O WELL DONE! I COMMEND YOUR PAINS; AND EVERY ONE SHALL SHARE IN THE GAINS;
AND NOW ABOUT THE CAULDRON SING, LIVE ELVES AND FAIRIES IN A RING, ENCHANTING ALL THAT YOU PUT IN!
BY THE PRICKING OF MY THUMBS, SOMETHING WICKED THIS WAY COMES! **OPEN, LOCKS, WHOEVER KNOCKS!**

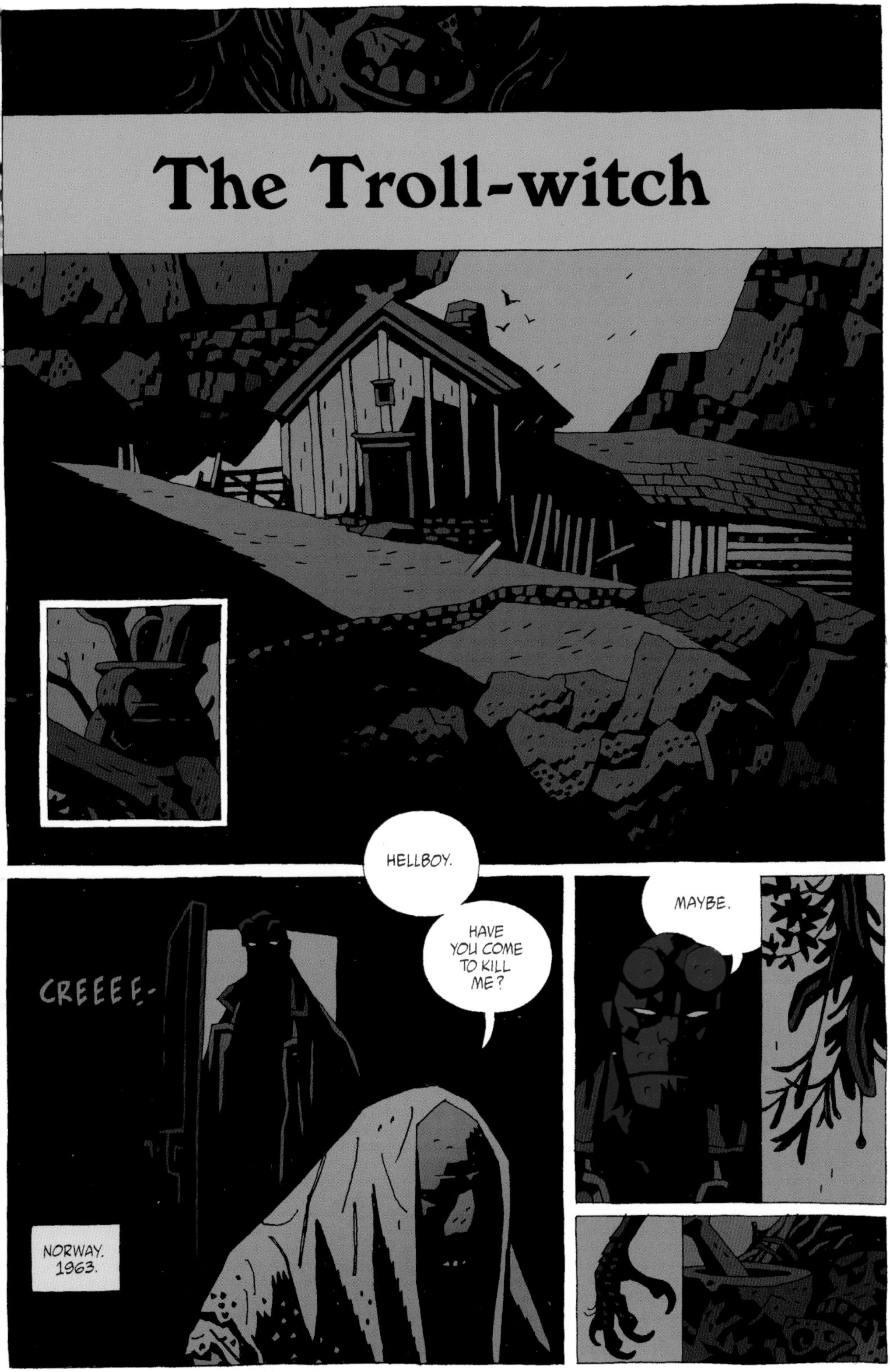
The Troll-witch
CREEEE-
NORWAY. 1963.
HELLBOY.
HAVE YOU COME TO KILL ME?
MAYBE.

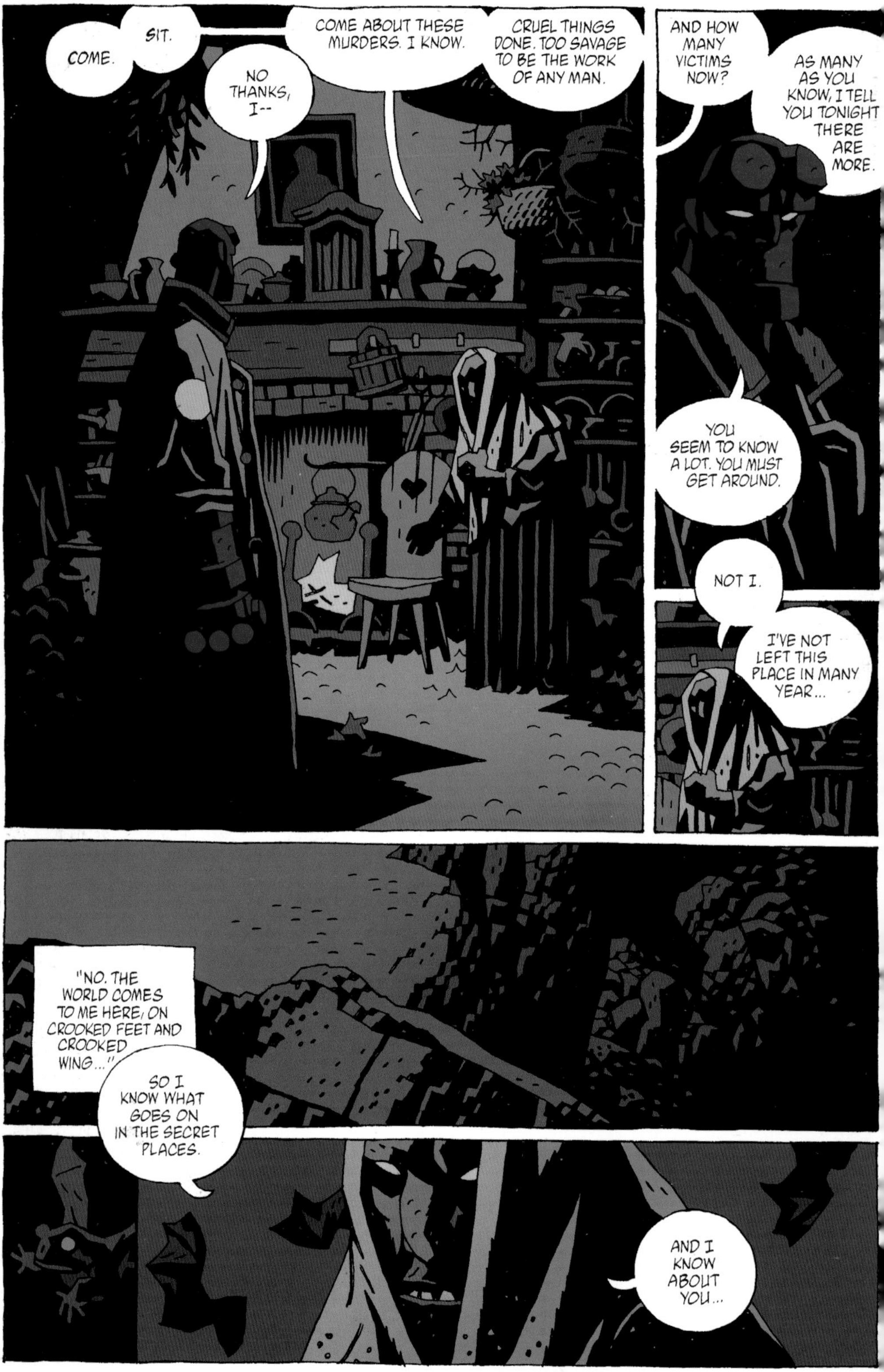
COME.
SIT.
NO THANKS, I--
COME ABOUT THESE MURDERS. I KNOW.
CRUEL THINGS DONE. TOO SAVAGE TO BE THE WORK OF ANY MAN.
AND HOW MANY VICTIMS NOW?
AS MANY AS YOU KNOW, I TELL YOU TONIGHT THERE ARE MORE.
YOU SEEM TO KNOW A LOT. YOU MUST GET AROUND.
NOT I.
I'VE NOT LEFT THIS PLACE IN MANY YEAR...
"NO. THE WORLD COMES TO ME HERE, ON CROOKED FEET AND CROOKED WING..."
SO I KNOW WHAT GOES ON IN THE SECRET PLACES.
AND I KNOW ABOUT YOU...

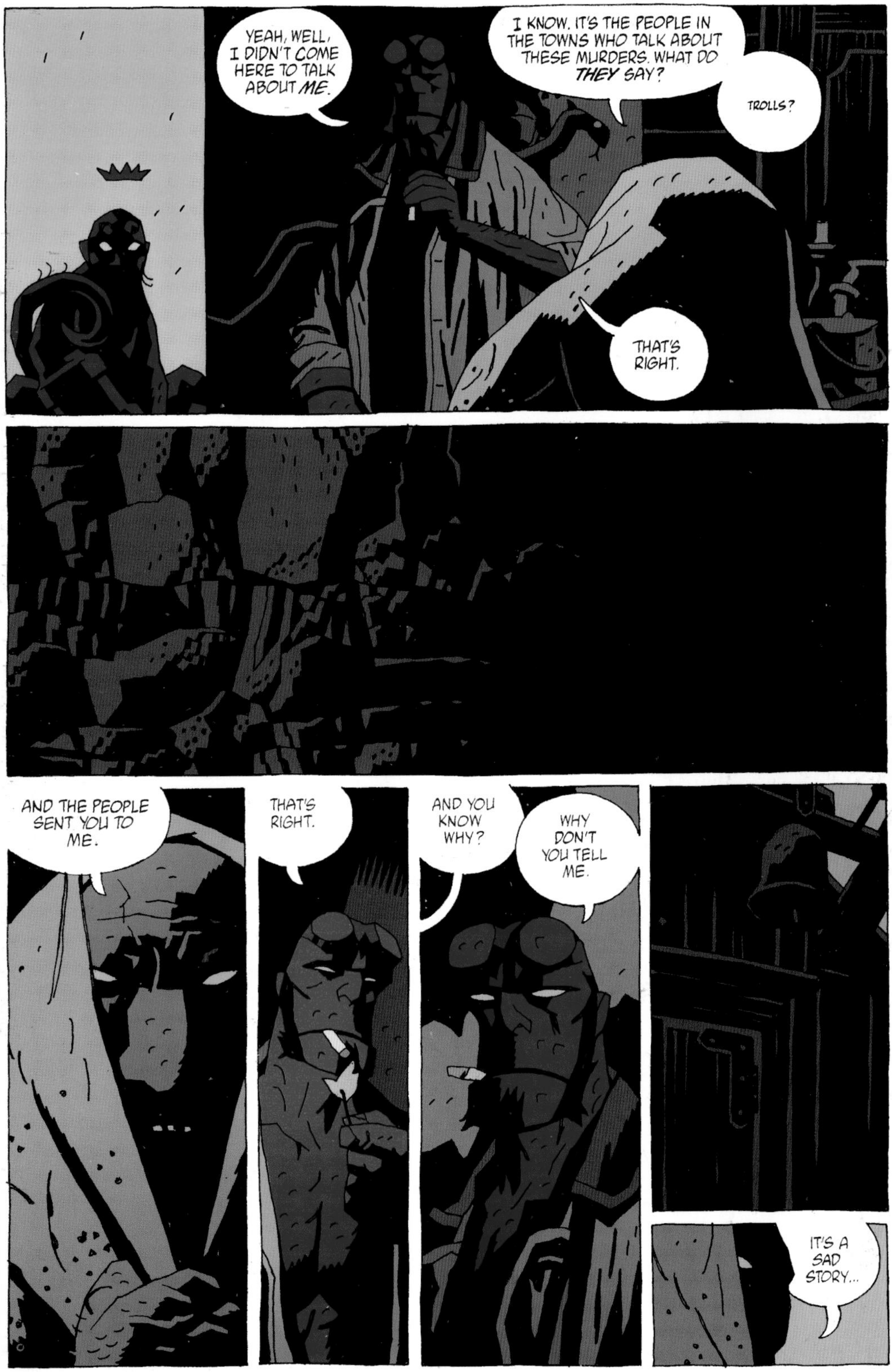
YEAH, WELL, I DIDN'T COME HERE TO TALK ABOUT *ME*.
I KNOW. IT'S THE PEOPLE IN THE TOWNS WHO TALK ABOUT THESE MURDERS. WHAT DO *THEY* SAY?
TROLLS?
THAT'S RIGHT.
AND THE PEOPLE SENT YOU TO ME.
THAT'S RIGHT.
AND YOU KNOW WHY?
WHY DON'T YOU TELL ME.
IT'S A SAD STORY...

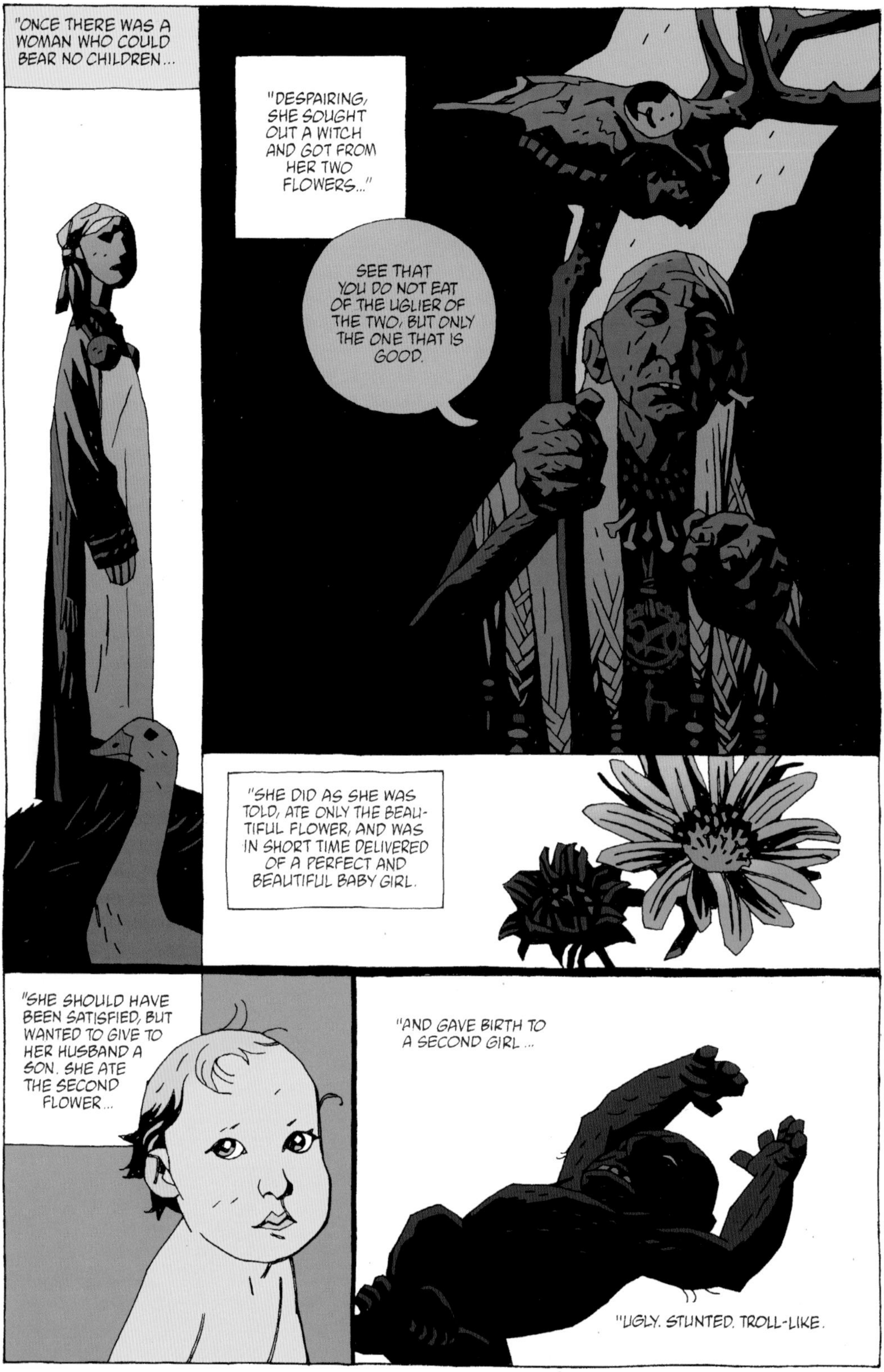
"ONCE THERE WAS A WOMAN WHO COULD BEAR NO CHILDREN...
"DESPAIRING, SHE SOUGHT OUT A WITCH AND GOT FROM HER TWO FLOWERS..."
SEE THAT YOU DO NOT EAT OF THE UGLIER OF THE TWO, BUT ONLY THE ONE THAT IS GOOD.
"SHE DID AS SHE WAS TOLD, ATE ONLY THE BEAUTIFUL FLOWER, AND WAS IN SHORT TIME DELIVERED OF A PERFECT AND BEAUTIFUL BABY GIRL.
"SHE SHOULD HAVE BEEN SATISFIED, BUT WANTED TO GIVE TO HER HUSBAND A SON. SHE ATE THE SECOND FLOWER...
"AND GAVE BIRTH TO A SECOND GIRL...
"UGLY. STUNTED. TROLL-LIKE.

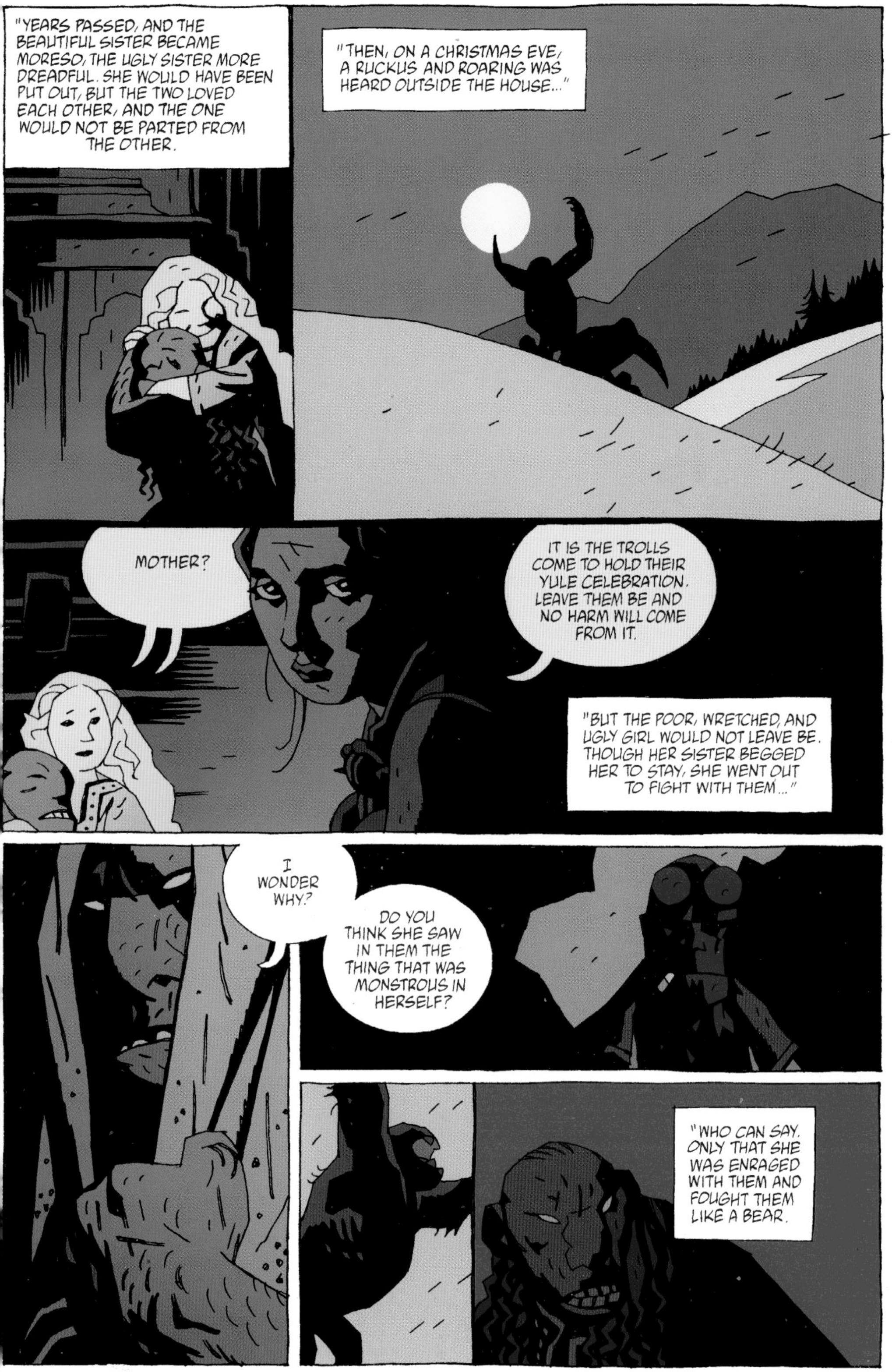
"YEARS PASSED, AND THE BEAUTIFUL SISTER BECAME MORESO, THE UGLY SISTER MORE DREADFUL. SHE WOULD HAVE BEEN PUT OUT, BUT THE TWO LOVED EACH OTHER, AND THE ONE WOULD NOT BE PARTED FROM THE OTHER.
"THEN, ON A CHRISTMAS EVE, A RUCKUS AND ROARING WAS HEARD OUTSIDE THE HOUSE..."
MOTHER?
IT IS THE TROLLS COME TO HOLD THEIR YULE CELEBRATION. LEAVE THEM BE AND NO HARM WILL COME FROM IT.
"BUT THE POOR, WRETCHED, AND UGLY GIRL WOULD NOT LEAVE BE. THOUGH HER SISTER BEGGED HER TO STAY, SHE WENT OUT TO FIGHT WITH THEM..."
I WONDER WHY?
DO YOU THINK SHE SAW IN THEM THE THING THAT WAS MONSTROUS IN HERSELF?
"WHO CAN SAY. ONLY THAT SHE WAS ENRAGED WITH THEM AND FOUGHT THEM LIKE A BEAR.

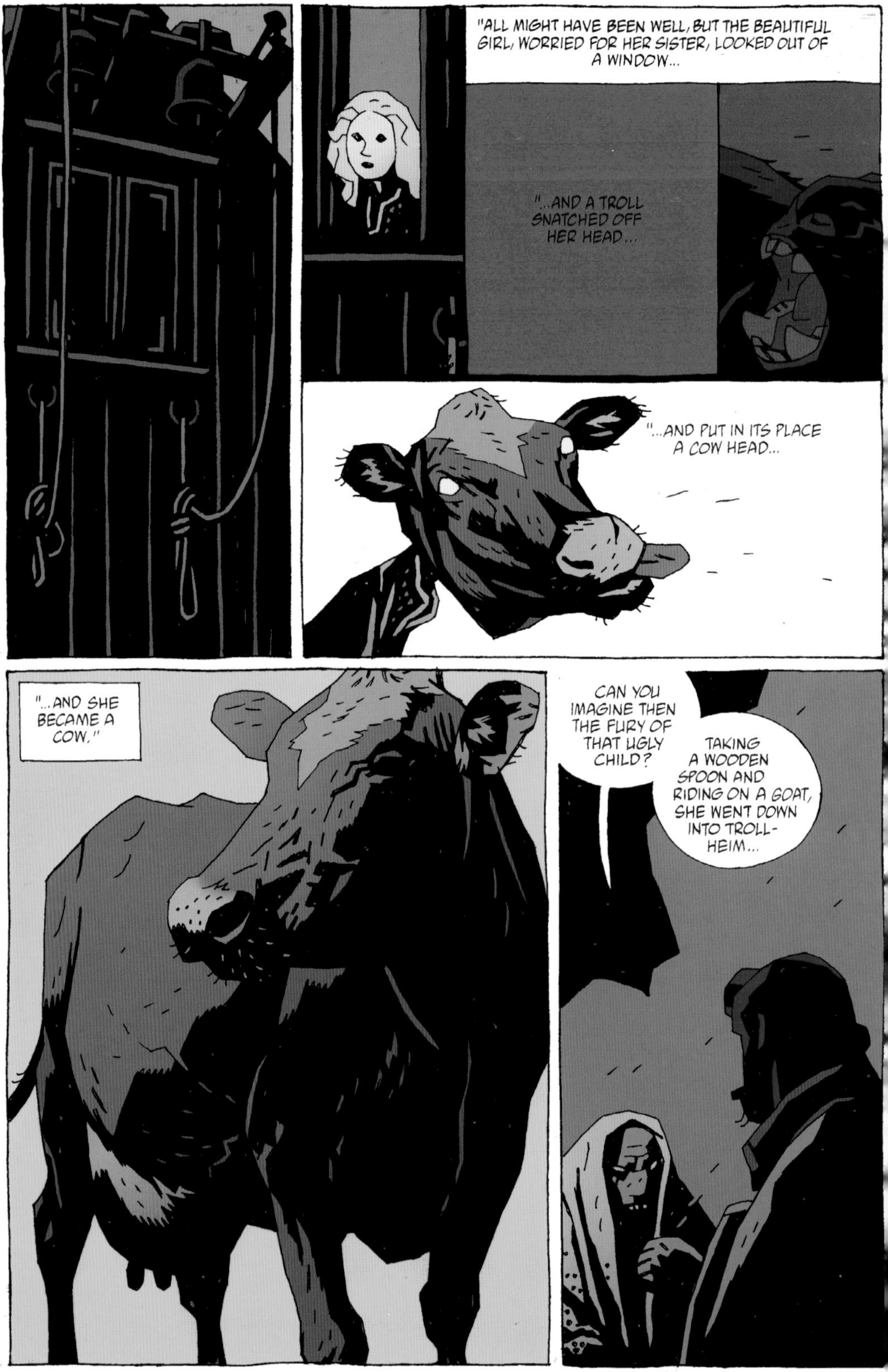
"ALL MIGHT HAVE BEEN WELL, BUT THE BEAUTIFUL GIRL, WORRIED FOR HER SISTER, LOOKED OUT OF A WINDOW...
"...AND A TROLL SNATCHED OFF HER HEAD...
"...AND PUT IN ITS PLACE A COW HEAD...
"...AND SHE BECAME A COW."
CAN YOU IMAGINE THEN THE FURY OF THAT UGLY CHILD?
TAKING A WOODEN SPOON AND RIDING ON A GOAT, SHE WENT DOWN INTO TROLL-HEIM...

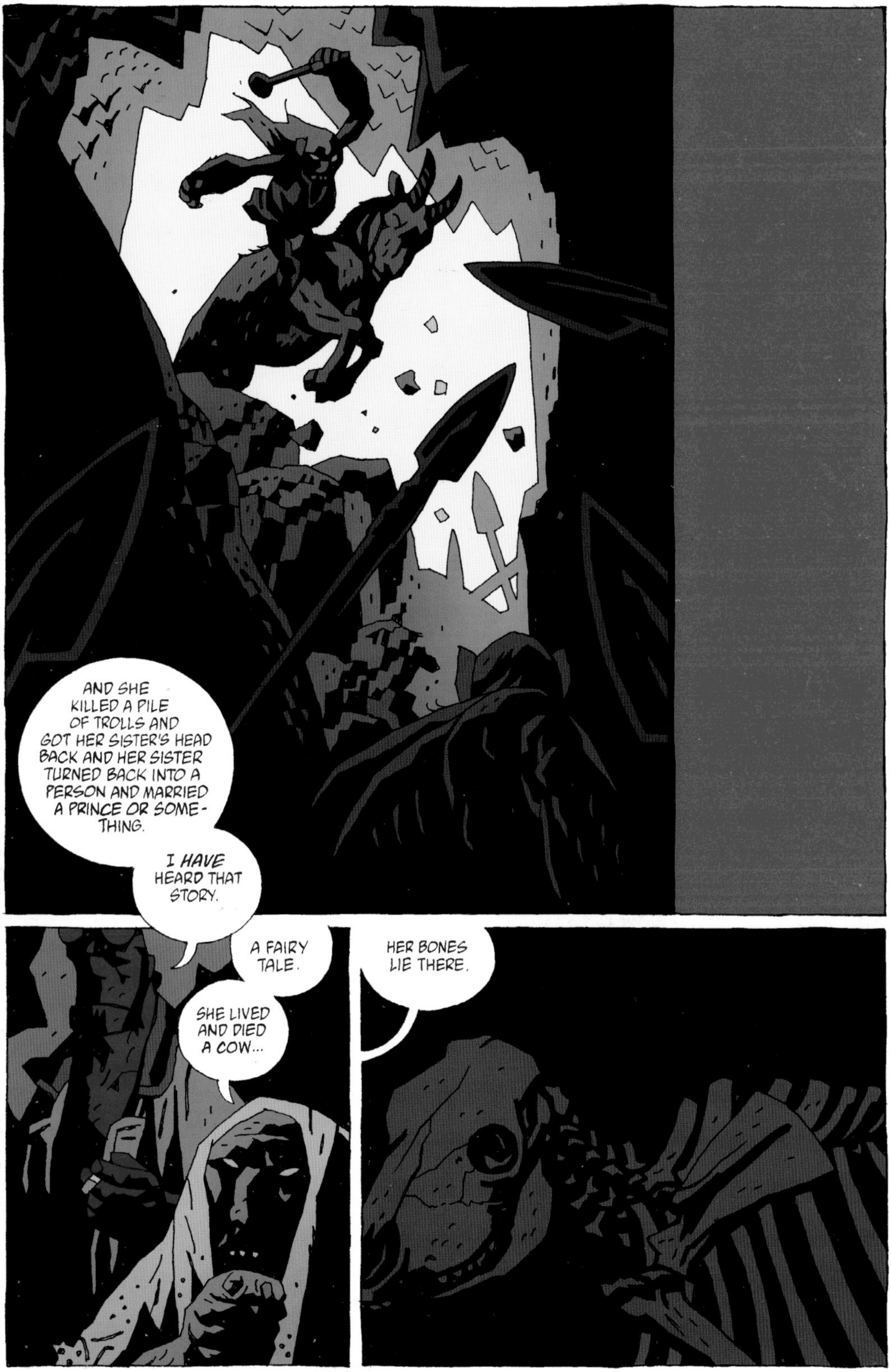
AND SHE KILLED A PILE OF TROLLS AND GOT HER SISTER'S HEAD BACK AND HER SISTER TURNED BACK INTO A PERSON AND MARRIED A PRINCE OR SOME-THING.
I *HAVE* HEARD THAT STORY.
A FAIRY TALE.
SHE LIVED AND DIED A COW...
HER BONES LIE THERE.

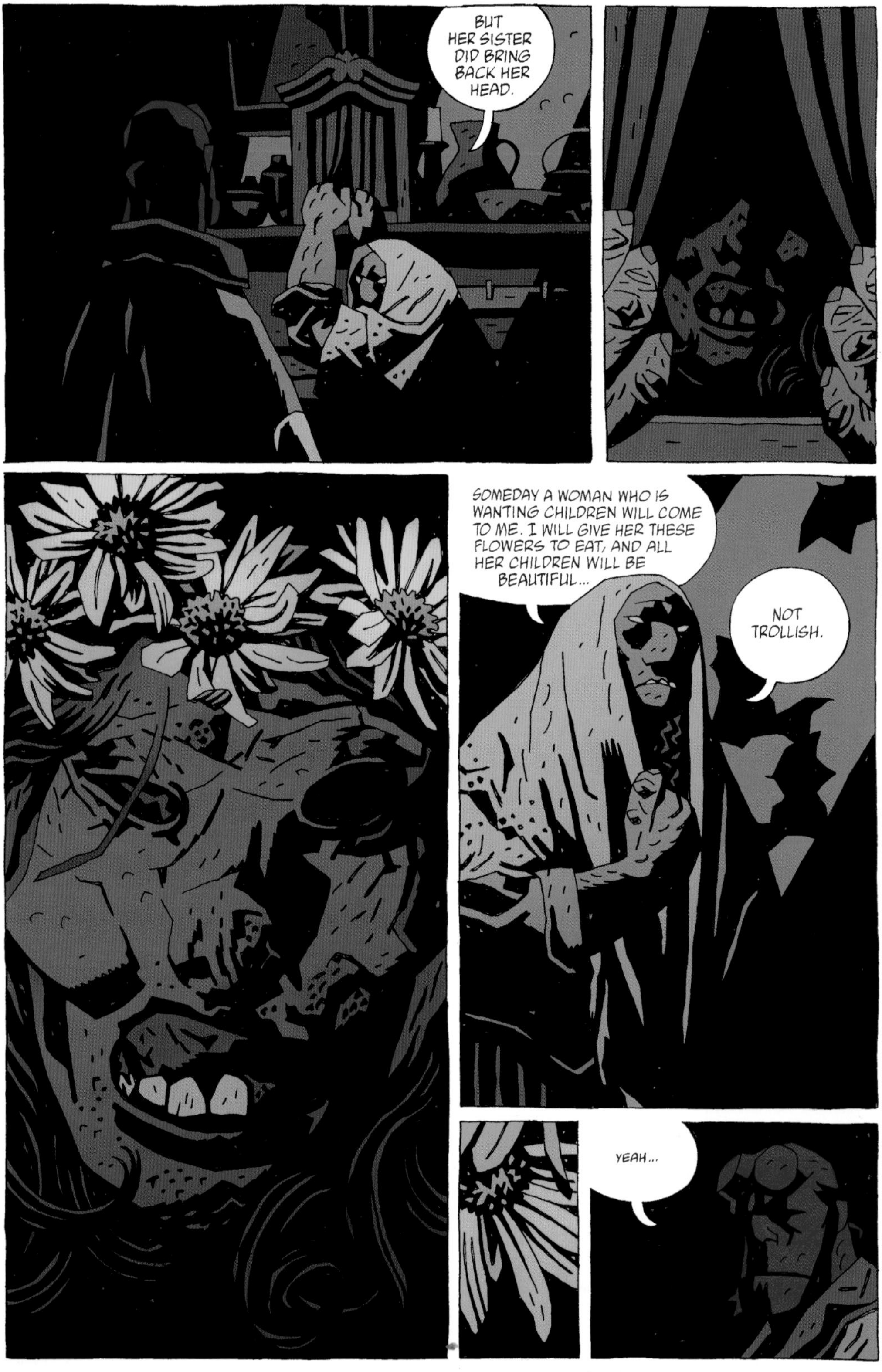
BUT HER SISTER DID BRING BACK HER HEAD.
SOMEDAY A WOMAN WHO IS WANTING CHILDREN WILL COME TO ME. I WILL GIVE HER THESE FLOWERS TO EAT, AND ALL HER CHILDREN WILL BE BEAUTIFUL...
NOT TROLLISH.
YEAH...

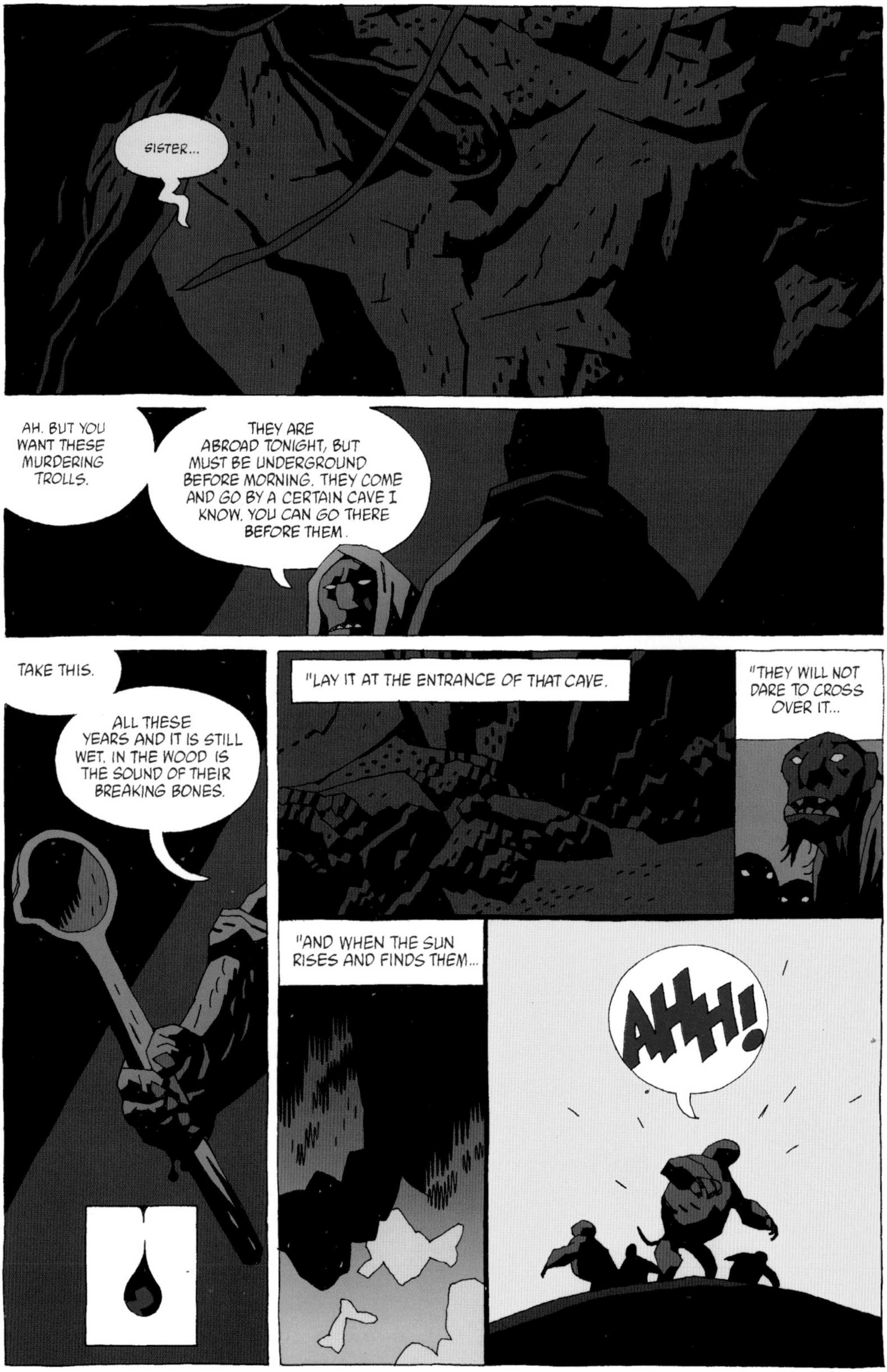
SISTER...
AH. BUT YOU WANT THESE MURDERING TROLLS.
THEY ARE ABROAD TONIGHT, BUT MUST BE UNDERGROUND BEFORE MORNING. THEY COME AND GO BY A CERTAIN CAVE I KNOW. YOU CAN GO THERE BEFORE THEM.
TAKE THIS.
ALL THESE YEARS AND IT IS STILL WET. IN THE WOOD IS THE SOUND OF THEIR BREAKING BONES.
"LAY IT AT THE ENTRANCE OF THAT CAVE.
"THEY WILL NOT DARE TO CROSS OVER IT...
"AND WHEN THE SUN RISES AND FINDS THEM...
AHH!

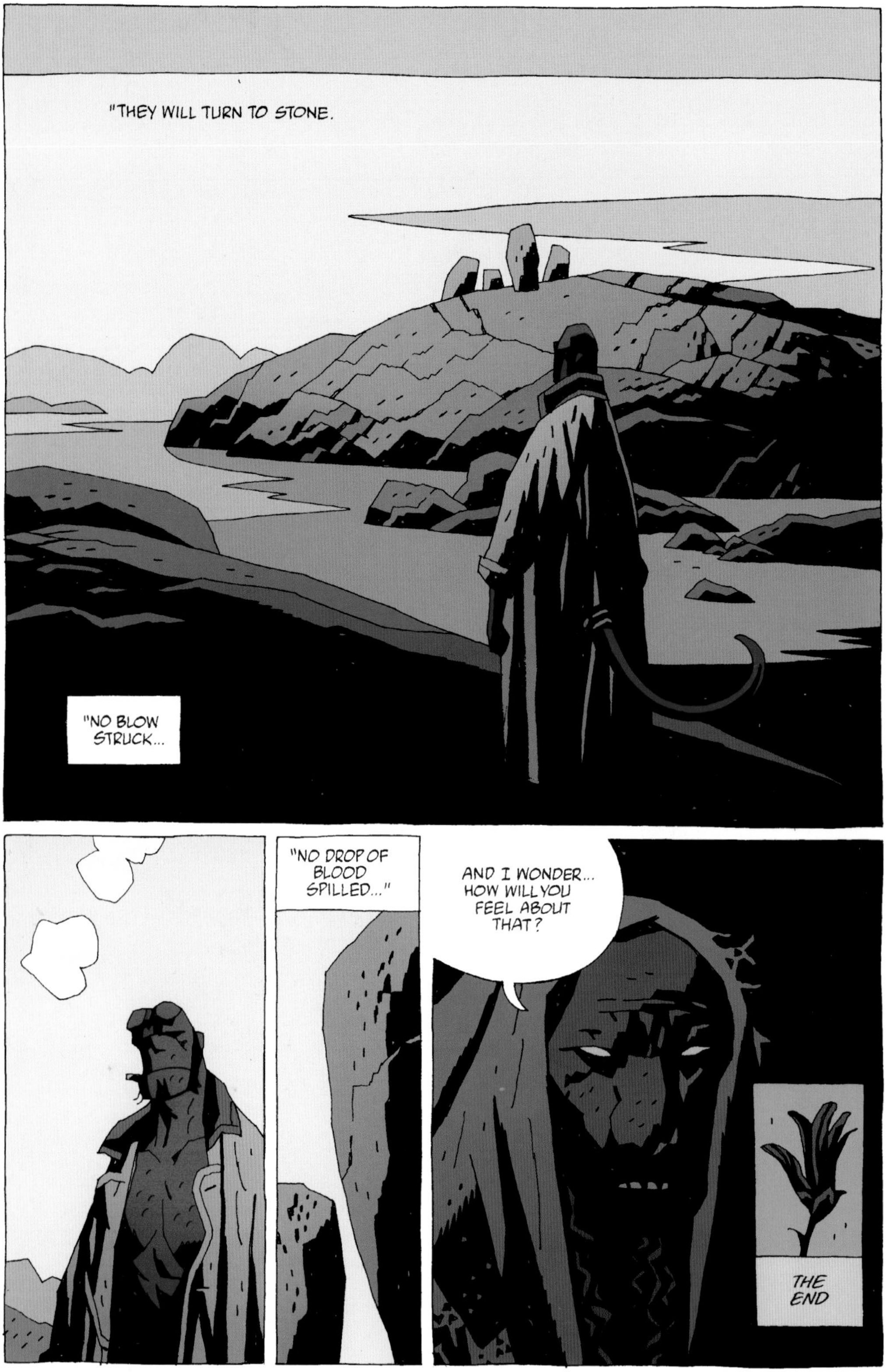
"THEY WILL TURN TO STONE.
"NO BLOW STRUCK...
"NO DROP OF BLOOD SPILLED..."
AND I WONDER... HOW WILL YOU FEEL ABOUT THAT?
THE END

Mother of Toads

by **CLARK ASHTON SMITH**

ILLUSTRATIONS *by* GARY GIANNI

Why must you always hurry away, my little one?"

The voice of Mére Antoinette, the witch, was an amorous croaking. She ogled Pierre, the apothecary's young apprentice, with eyes full-orbed and unblinking as those of a toad. The folds beneath her chin swelled like the throat of some great batrachian. Her huge breasts, pale as frog-bellies, bulged from her torn gown as she leaned toward him.

Pierre Baudin, as usual, gave no answer; and she came closer, till he saw in the hollow of those breasts a moisture glistening like the dew of marshes ... like the slime of some amphibian ... a moisture that seemed always to linger there.

Her voice, raucously coaxing, persisted. "Stay a while tonight, my pretty orphan. No one will miss you in the village. And your master will not mind." She pressed against him with shuddering folds of fat. With her short flat fingers, which gave almost the appearance of being webbed, she seized his hand and drew it to her bosom.

Pierre wrenched the hand away and drew back discreetly. Repelled, rather than abashed, he averted his eyes. The witch was more than twice his age, and her charms were too uncouth and unsavory to tempt him for an instant. Also, her repute was such as to have nullified the attractions of even a younger and fairer sorceress. Her witchcraft had made her feared among the peasantry of that remote province, where belief in spells and philters was still common. The people of Averoigne called her La Mère des Crapauds, The Mother of Toads, a name given for more than one reason. Toads swarmed innumerably about her hut; they were said to be her familiars, and dark tales were told concerning their relationship to the sorceress, and the duties they performed at her bidding. Such tales were all the more readily believed because of those batrachian features that had always been remarked in her aspect.

The youth disliked her, even as he disliked the sluggish, abnormally large toads on which he had sometimes trodden in the dusk, upon the path between her hut and the village of Les Hiboux. He could hear some of these creatures croaking now; and it seemed, weirdly, that they uttered half-articulate echoes of the witch's words.

It would be dark soon, he reflected. The path along the marshes was not pleasant by night, and he felt doubly anxious to depart. Still without replying to Mère Antoinette's invitation, he reached for the black triangular vial she had set before him on her greasy table. The vial contained a philter of curious potency which his master, Alain le Dindon, had sent him to procure. Le Dindon, the village apothecary, was wont to deal surreptitiously in certain dubious medicaments supplied by the witch, and Pierre had often gone on such errands to her osier-hidden hut.

The old apothecary, whose humor was rough and ribald, had sometimes rallied Pierre concerning Mère Antoinette's preference for him. "Some night, my lad, you will remain with her," he had said. "Be careful, or the big toad will crush you." Remembering this gibe, the boy flushed angrily as he turned to go.

"Stay," insisted Mère Antoinette. "The fog is cold on the marshes; and it thickens apace. I knew that you were coming, and I have mulled for you a goodly measure of the red wine of Ximes."

She removed the lid from an earthen pitcher and poured its steaming contents into a large cup. The purplish-red wine creamed delectably, and an odor of hot, delicious spices filled the hut, overpowering the less agreeable odors from the simmering cauldron, the half-dried newts, vipers, bat wings, and evil, nauseous herbs hanging on the walls, and the reek of the black candles of pitch and corpse-tallow that burned always, by noon or night, in that murky interior.

"I'll drink it," said Pierre, a little grudgingly. "That is, if it contains nothing of your own concoction."

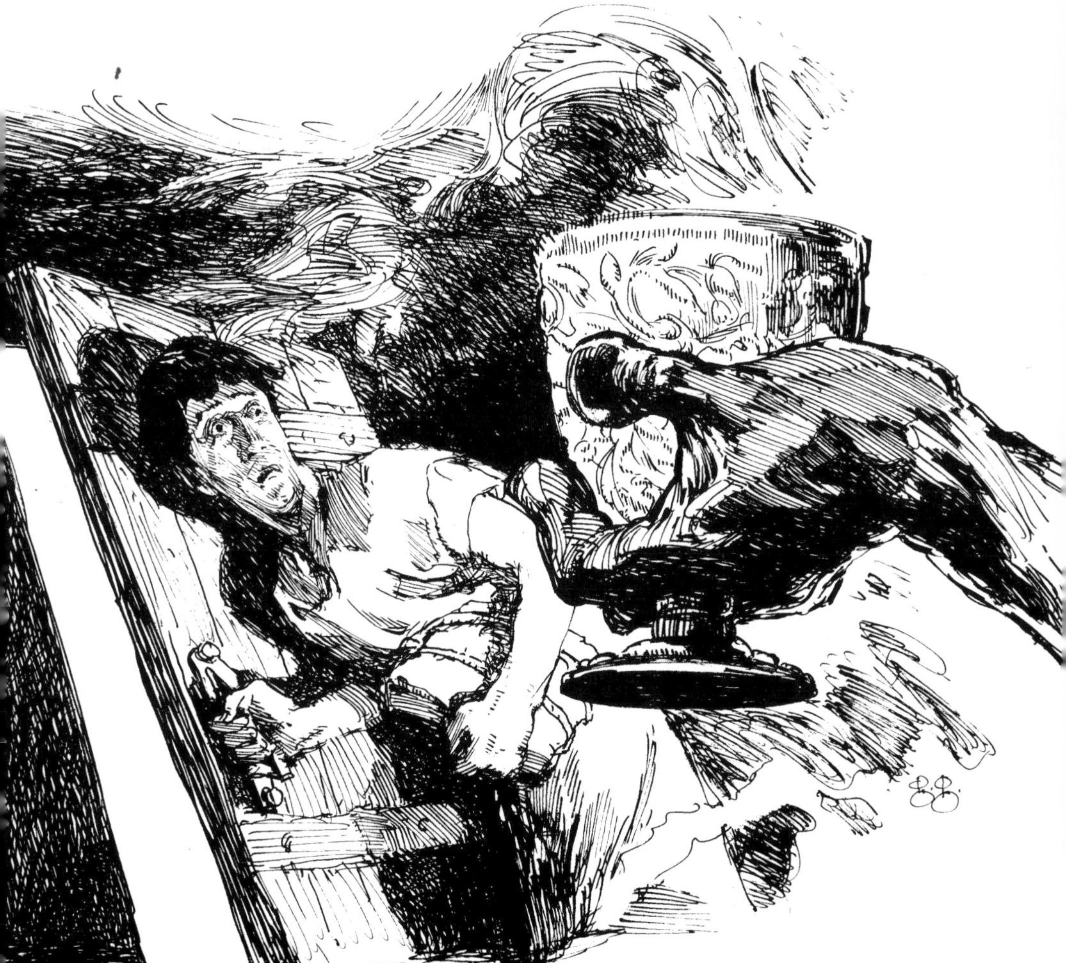

"'Tis naught but sound wine, four seasons old, with spices of Arabia," the sorceress croaked ingratiatingly. "'Twill warm your stomach and ..." She added something inaudible as Pierre accepted the cup.

Before drinking, he inhaled the fumes of the beverage with some caution but was reassured by its pleasant smell. Surely it was innocent of any drug, any philter brewed by the witch, for, to his knowledge, her preparations were all evil-smelling.

Still, as if warned by some premonition, he hesitated. Then he remembered that the sunset air was indeed chill, that mists had gathered furtively behind him as he came to Mére Antoinette's dwelling. The wine would fortify him for the dismal return walk to Les Hiboux. He quaffed it quickly and set down the cup.

"Truly, it is good wine," he declared. "But I must go now."

Even as he spoke, he felt in his stomach and veins the spreading warmth of the alcohol, of the spices ... of something more ardent than these. It seemed that his voice was unreal and strange, falling as if from a height above him. The warmth grew, mounting within him like a golden flame fed by magic oils. His blood, a seething torrent, poured tumultuously and more tumultuously through his members.

There was a deep soft thundering in his ears, a rosy dazzlement in his eyes. Somehow the hut appeared to expand, to change luminously about him. He hardly recognized its squalid furnishings, its litter of baleful oddments, on which a torrid splendor was shed by the black candles, tipped with ruddy fire, that towered and swelled gigantically into the soft gloom. His blood burned as with the throbbing flame of the candles.

It came to him, for an instant, that all this was a questionable enchantment, a glamour wrought by the witch's wine. Fear was upon him and he wished to flee. Then, close beside him, he saw Mére Antoinette.

Briefly he marveled at the change that had befallen her. Then fear and wonder were alike forgotten, together with his old repulsion. He knew why the magic warmth mounted ever higher and hotter within him; why his flesh glowed like the ruddy tapers.

The soiled skirt she had worn lay at her feet, and she stood naked as Lilith, the first witch. The lumpish limbs and body had grown voluptuous; the pale, thick-lipped mouth enticed him with a promise of ampler kisses than other mouths could yield. The pits of her short round arms, the concave of her ponderously drooping breasts, the heavy creases and swollen rondures of flanks and thighs, all were fraught with luxurious allurement.

"Do you like me now, my little one?" she questioned.

This time he did not draw away but met her with hot, questing hands when she pressed heavily against him. Her limbs were cool and moist; her

breasts yielded like the turf-mounds above a bog. Her body was white and
wholly hairless, but here and there he found curious roughnesses ... like
those on the skin of a toad ... that somehow sharpened his desire instead of
repelling it.

She was so huge that his fingers barely joined behind her. His two
hands, together, were equal only to the cupping of a single breast. But the
wine had filled his blood with a philterous ardor.

She led him to her couch beside the hearth where a great cauldron
boiled mysteriously, sending up its fumes in strange-twining coils that
suggested vague and obscene figures. The couch was rude and bare. But the
flesh of the sorceress was like deep, luxurious cushions ...

Pierre awoke in the ashy dawn, when the tall black tapers had dwindled
down and had melted limply in their sockets. Sick and confused, he sought
vainly to remember where he was or what he had done. Then, turning a
little, he saw beside him on the couch a thing that was like some impossible
monster of ill dreams: a toadlike form, large as a fat woman. Its limbs were

somehow like a woman's arms and legs. Its pale, warty body pressed and bulged against him, and he felt the rounded softness of something that resembled a breast.

Nausea rose within him as memory of that delirious night returned. Most foully he had been beguiled by the witch, and had succumbed to her evil enchantments.

It seemed that an incubus smothered him, weighing upon all his limbs and body. He shut his eyes, that he might no longer behold the loathsome thing that was Mére Antoinette in her true semblance. Slowly, with prodigious effort, he drew himself away from the crushing nightmare shape. It did not stir or appear to waken, and he slid quickly from the couch.

Again, compelled by a noisome fascination, he peered at the thing on the couch—and saw only the gross form of Mére Antoinette. Perhaps his impression of a great toad beside him had been but an illusion, a half-dream that lingered after slumber. He lost something of his nightmarish horror, but his gorge still rose in a sick disgust, remembering the lewdness to which he had yielded.

Fearing that the witch might awaken at any moment and seek to detain him, he stole noiselessly from the hut. It was broad daylight, but a cold, hueless mist lay everywhere, shrouding the reedy marshes, and hanging like a ghostly curtain on the path he must follow to Les Hiboux. Moving and seething always, the mist seemed to reach toward him with intercepting fingers as he started homeward. He shivered at its touch, he bowed his head and drew his cloak closer around him.

Thicker and thicker the mist swirled, coiling, writhing endlessly, as if to bar Pierre's progress. He could discern the twisting, narrow path for only a few paces in advance. It was hard to find the familiar landmarks, hard to recognize the osiers and willows that loomed suddenly before him like gray phantoms and faded again into the white nothingness as he went onward. Never had he seen such fog: it was like the blinding, stifling fumes of a thousand witch-stirred cauldrons.

Though he was not altogether sure of his surroundings, Pierre thought that he had covered half the distance to the village. Then, all at once, he began to meet the toads. They were hidden by the mist till he came close upon them. Misshapen, unnaturally big and bloated, they squatted in his way on the little footpath or hopped sluggishly from the pallid gloom on either hand.

Several struck against his feet with a horrible and heavy flopping. He stepped unaware upon one of them, and slipped in the squashy putrescence it had made, barely saving himself from a headlong fall on the bog's rim. Black, miry water gloomed close beside him as he staggered there.

Turning to regain his path, he crushed others of the toads to an abhorrent pulp under his feet. The marshy soil was alive with them. They

28

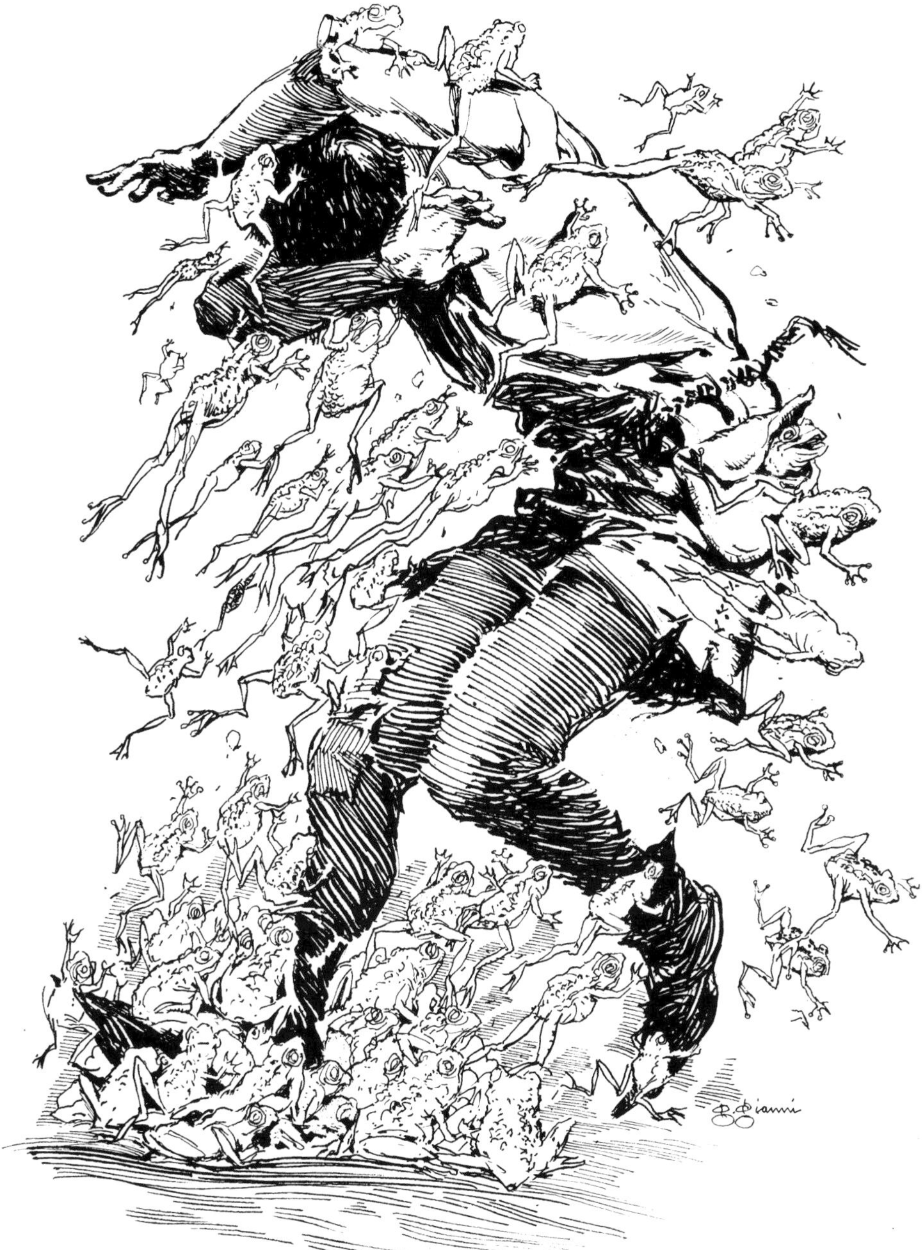

flopped against him from the mist, striking his legs, his bosom, his very face with their clammy bodies. They rose up by scores like a devil-driven legion. It seemed that there was a malignance, an evil purpose in their movements, in the buffeting of their violent impact. He could make no progress on the swarming path, but lurched to and fro, slipping blindly, and shielding his face with lifted hands. He felt an eerie consternation, an eldritch horror. It was as if the nightmare of his awakening in the witch's hut had somehow returned upon him.

The toads came always from the direction of Les Hiboux, as if to drive him back toward Mére Antoinette's dwelling. They bounded against him, like a monstrous hail, like missiles flung by unseen demons. The ground was covered by them; the air was filled with their hurtling bodies. Once, he nearly went down beneath them.

Their number seemed to increase, they pelted him in a noxious storm. He gave way before them, his courage broke, and he started to run at random, without knowing that he had left the safe path. Losing all thought of direction in his frantic desire to escape from those impossible myriads, he plunged on amid the dim reeds and sedges, over ground that quivered gelatinously beneath him. Always at his heels he heard the soft, heavy

flopping of the toads; and sometimes they rose up like a sudden wall to bar his way and turn him aside. More than once, they drove him back from the verge of hidden quagmires into which he would otherwise have fallen. It was as if they were herding him deliberately and concertedly to a destined goal.

Now, like the lifting of a dense curtain, the mist rolled away, and Pierre saw before him in a golden dazzle of morning sunshine the green, thick-growing osiers that surrounded Mére Antoinette's hut. The toads had all disappeared, though he could have sworn that hundreds of them were hopping close about him an instant previously. With a feeling of helpless fright and panic, he knew that he was still within the witch's toils; that the toads were indeed her familiars, as so many people believed them to be. They had prevented his escape, and had brought him back to the foul creature ... whether woman, batrachian, or both ... who was known as The Mother of Toads.

Pierre's sensations were those of one who sinks momently deeper into some black and bottomless quicksand. He saw the witch emerge from the hut and come toward him. Her thick fingers, with pale folds of skin between them like the beginnings of a web, were stretched and flattened on the steaming cup that she carried. A sudden gust of wind arose as if from nowhere, lifting the scanty skirts of Mére Antoinette about her fat thighs, and bearing to Pierre's nostrils the hot, familiar spices of the drugged wine. "Why did you leave so hastily, my little one?" There was an amorous wheedling in the very tone of the witch's question. "I should not have let you go without another cup of the good red wine, mulled and spiced for the warming of your stomach ... See, I have prepared it for you ... knowing that you would return."

She came very close to him as she spoke, leering and sidling, and held the cup toward his lips. Pierre grew dizzy with the strange fumes and turned his head away. It seemed that a paralyzing spell had seized his muscles, for the simple movement required an immense effort.

His mind, however, was still clear, and the sick revulsion of that nightmare dawn returned upon him. He saw again the great toad that had lain at his side when he awakened.

"I will not drink your wine," he said firmly. "You are a foul witch, and I loathe you. Let me go."

"Why do you loathe me?" croaked Mére Antoinette. "You loved me yesternight. I can give you all that other women give ... and more."

"You are not a woman," said Pierre. "You are a big toad. I saw you in your true shape this morning. I'd rather drown in the marsh waters than sleep with you again."

An indescribable change came upon the sorceress before Pierre had finished speaking. The leer slid from her thick and pallid features, leaving them blankly inhuman for an instant. Then her eyes bulged and goggled horribly, and her whole body appeared to swell as if inflated with venom.

"Go, then!" she spat with a guttural virulence. "But you will soon wish that you had stayed ..."

The queer paralysis had lifted from Pierre's muscles. It was as if the injunction of the angry witch had served to revoke an insidious, half-woven spell. With no parting glance or word, Pierre turned from her and fled with long, hasty steps, almost running, on the path to Les Hiboux.

He had gone little more than a hundred paces when the fog began to return. It coiled shoreward in vast volumes from the marshes, it poured like smoke from the very ground at his feet. Almost instantly, the sun dimmed to a wan silver disk and disappeared. The blue heavens were lost in the pale and seething voidness overhead. The path before Pierre was blotted out till he seemed to walk on the sheer rim of a white abyss that moved with him as he went.

Like the clammy arms of specters, with death-chill fingers that clutched and caressed, the weird mists drew closer still about Pierre. They thickened in his nostrils and throat, they dripped in a heavy dew from his garments.

They choked him with the fetor of rank
waters and putrescent ooze ... and a stench
as of liquefying corpses that had risen
somewhere to the surface amid the fen.

Then, from the blank whiteness, the
toads assailed Pierre in a surging, solid wave
that towered above his head and swept him
from the dim path with the force of failing
seas as it descended. He went down,
splashing and floundering, into water that
swarmed with the numberless batrachians.
Thick slime was in his mouth and nose as he
struggled to regain his footing. The water,
however, was only knee-deep, and the
bottom, though slippery and oozy,
supported him with little yielding when he
stood erect.

He discerned indistinctly through the
mist the nearby margin from which he had
fallen. But his steps were weirdly and
horribly hampered by the toad-seething
waters when he strove to reach it. Inch by
inch, with a hopeless panic deepening upon
him, he fought toward the solid shore. The
toads leaped and tumbled about him with a
dizzying eddylike motion. They swirled like a
viscid undertow around his feet and shins.
They swept and swelled in great loathsome
undulations against his retarded knees.

However, he made slow and painful
progress, till his outstretched fingers could
almost grasp the wiry sedges that trailed
from the low bank. Then, from that mist-
bound shore, there fell and broke upon him
a second deluge of those demoniac toads;
and Pierre was borne helplessly backward
into the filthy waters.

Held down by the piling and crawling
masses, and drowning in nauseous darkness
at the thick-oozed bottom, he clawed feebly
at his assailants. For a moment, ere oblivion

came, his fingers found among them the outlines of a monstrous form that was somehow toadlike ... but large and heavy as a fat woman. At the last, it seemed to him that two enormous breasts were crushed closely down upon his face.

The End

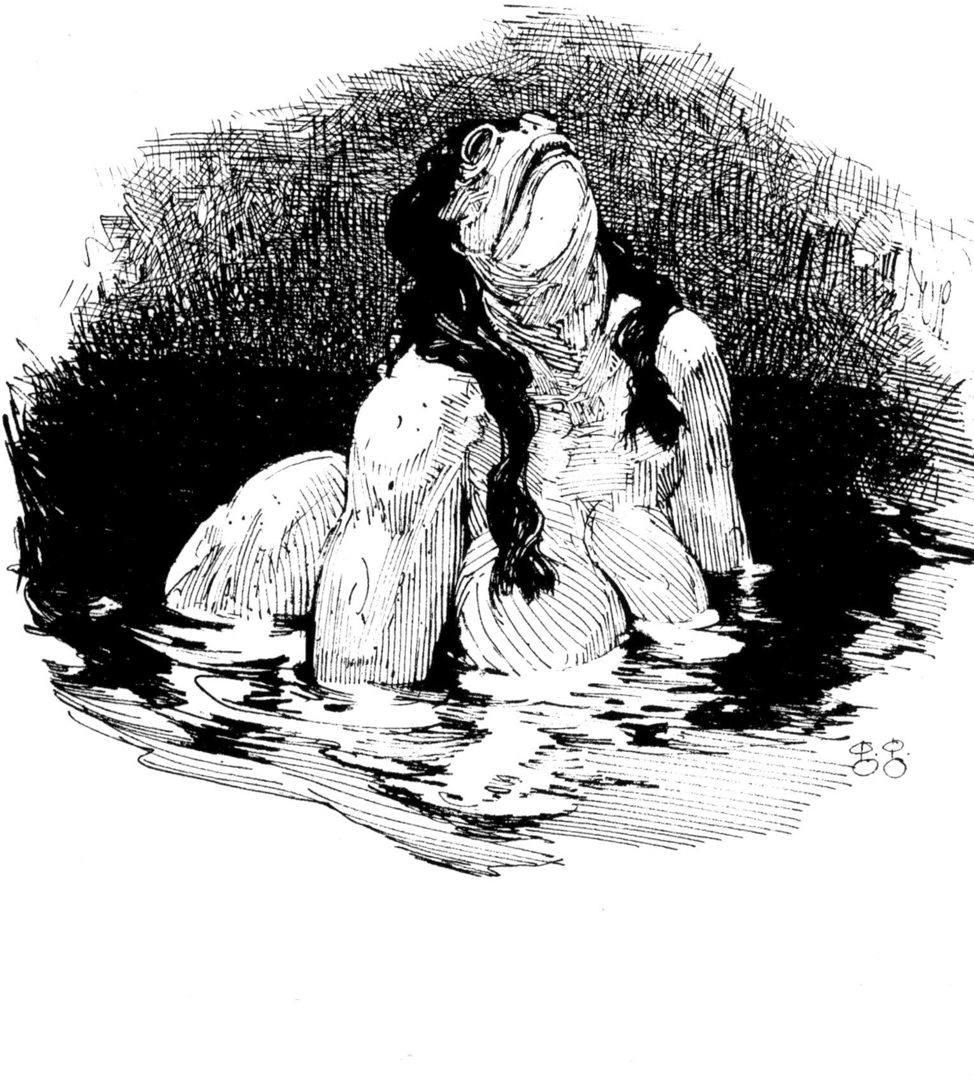

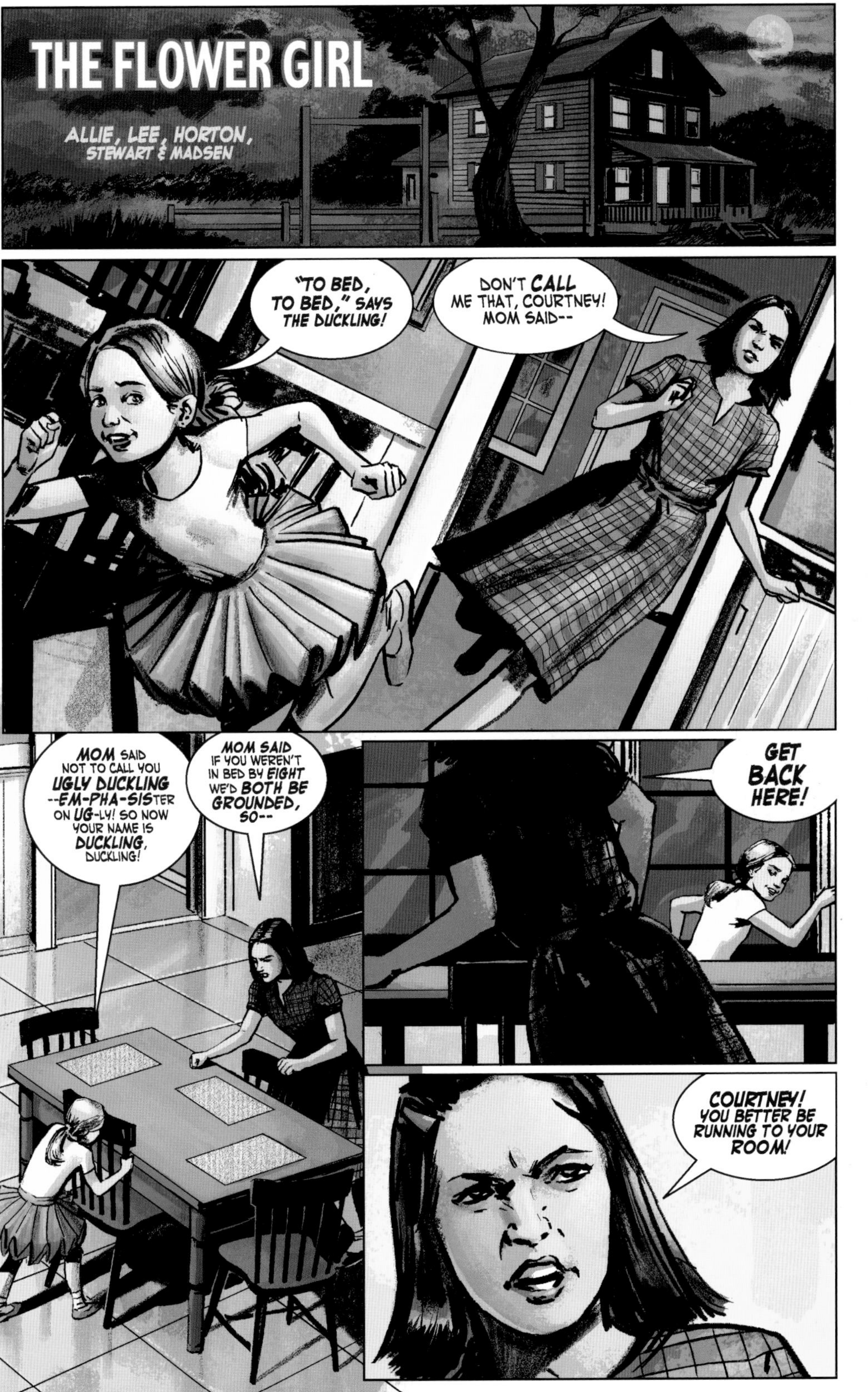
THE FLOWER GIRL
ALLIE, LEE, HORTON, STEWART & MADSEN
"TO BED, TO BED," SAYS THE DUCKLING!
DON'T CALL ME THAT, COURTNEY! MOM SAID--
MOM SAID NOT TO CALL YOU UGLY DUCKLING --EM-PHA-SIS-TER ON UG-LY! SO NOW YOUR NAME IS DUCKLING, DUCKLING!
MOM SAID IF YOU WEREN'T IN BED BY EIGHT WE'D BOTH BE GROUNDED, SO--
GET BACK HERE!
COURTNEY! YOU BETTER BE RUNNING TO YOUR ROOM!

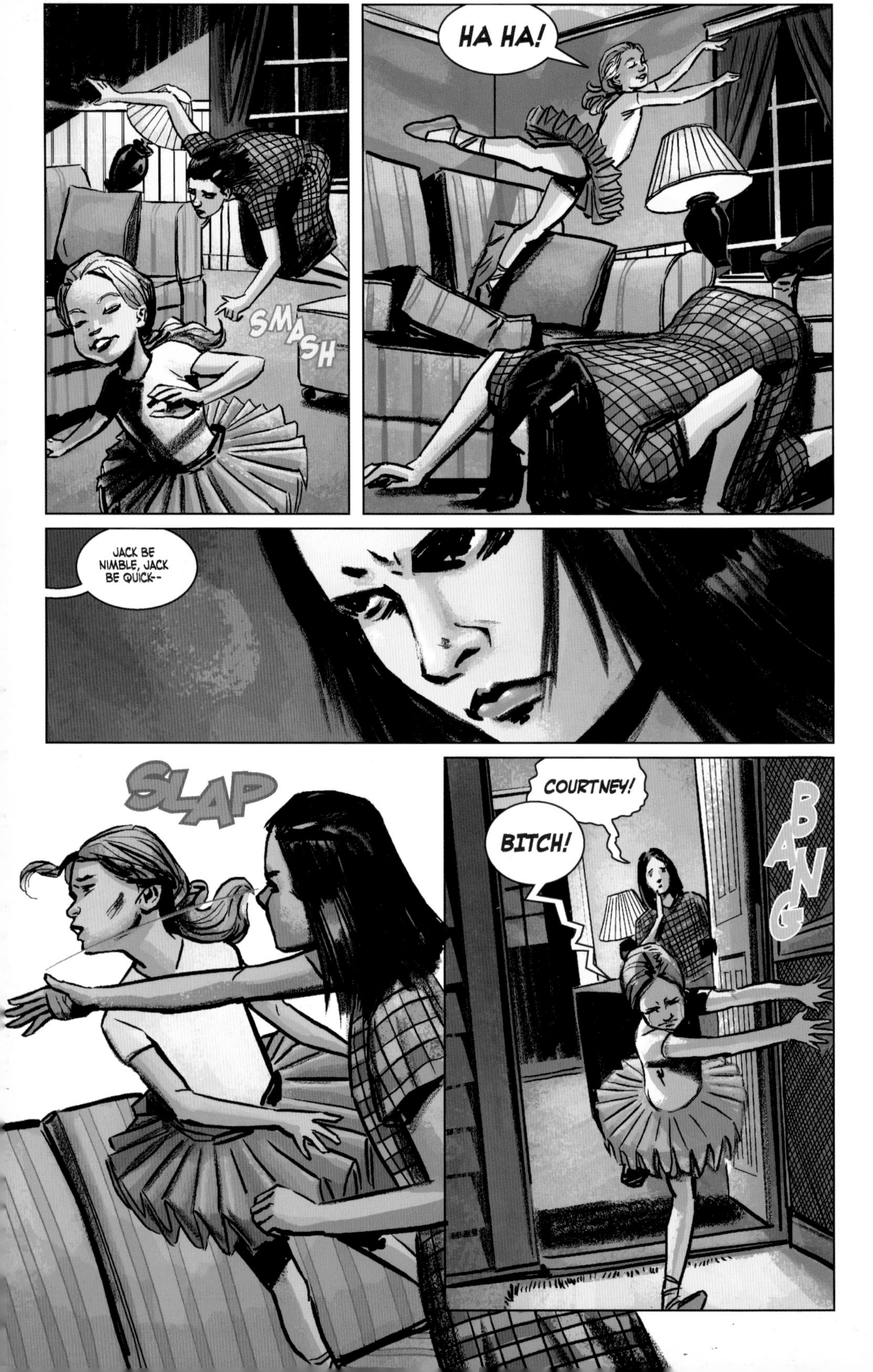
SMASH
HA HA!
JACK BE NIMBLE, JACK BE QUICK--
SLAP
COURTNEY!
BITCH!
BANG

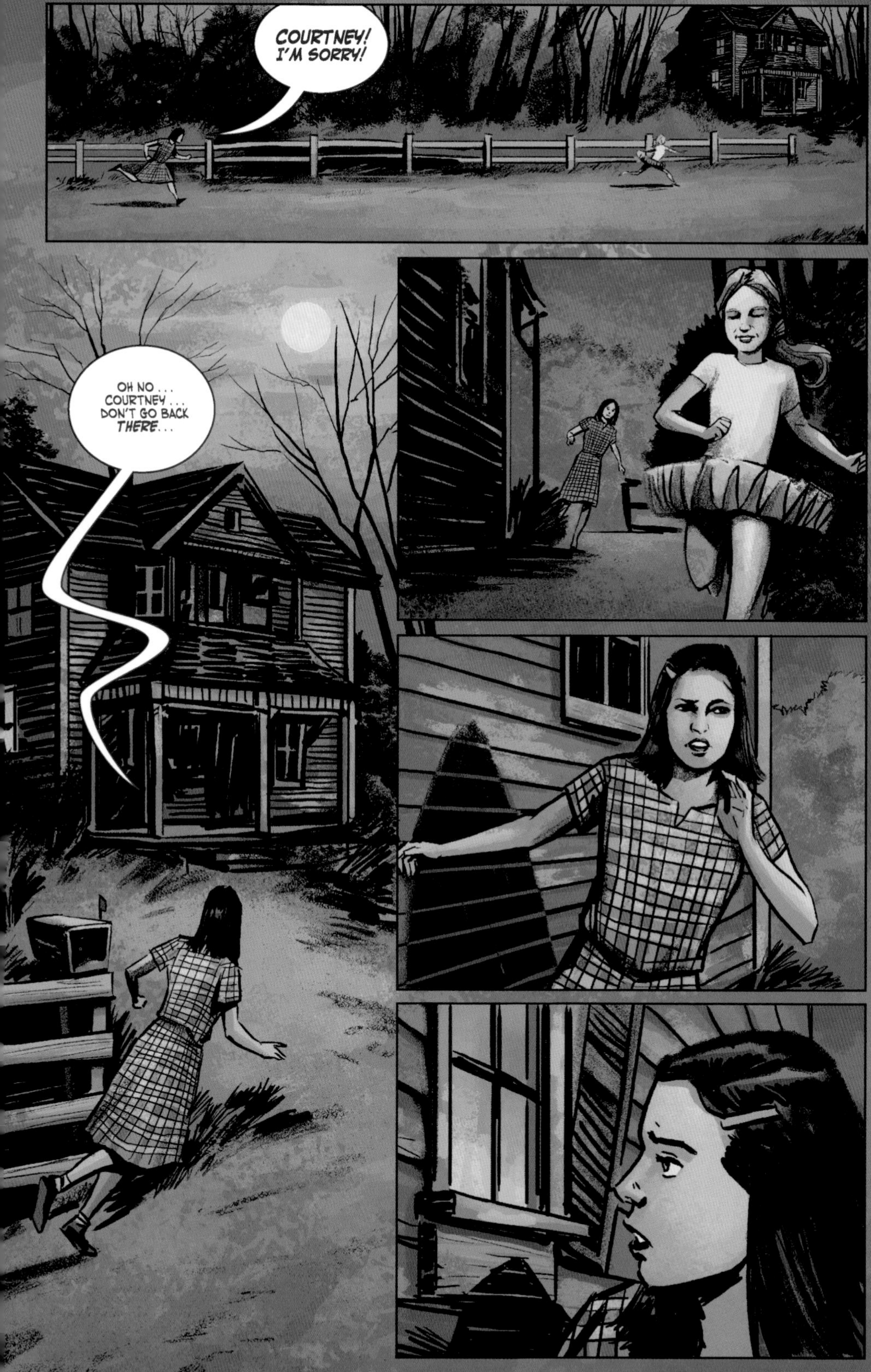
COURTNEY! I'M SORRY!
OH NO . . . COURTNEY . . . DON'T GO BACK THERE . . .

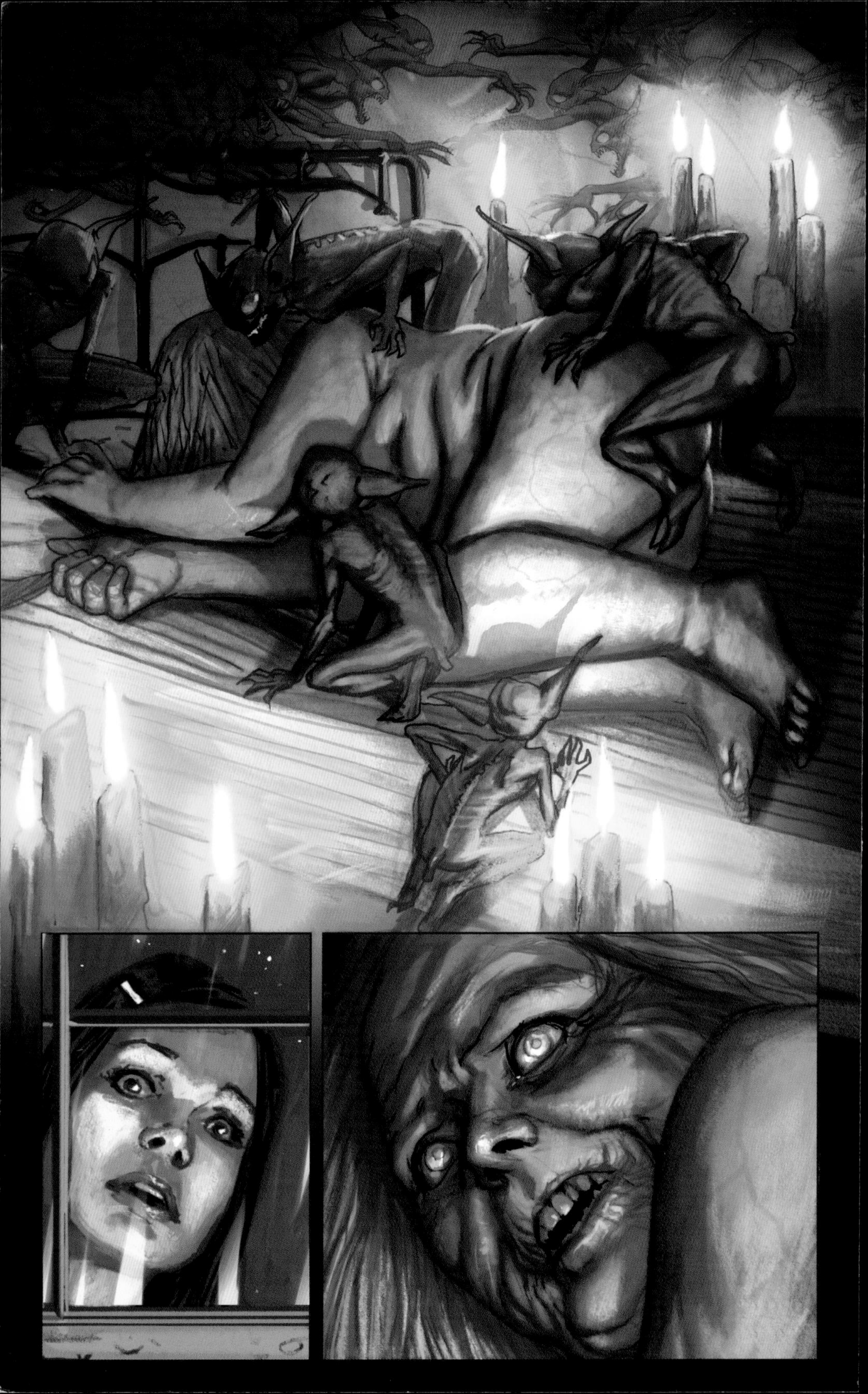

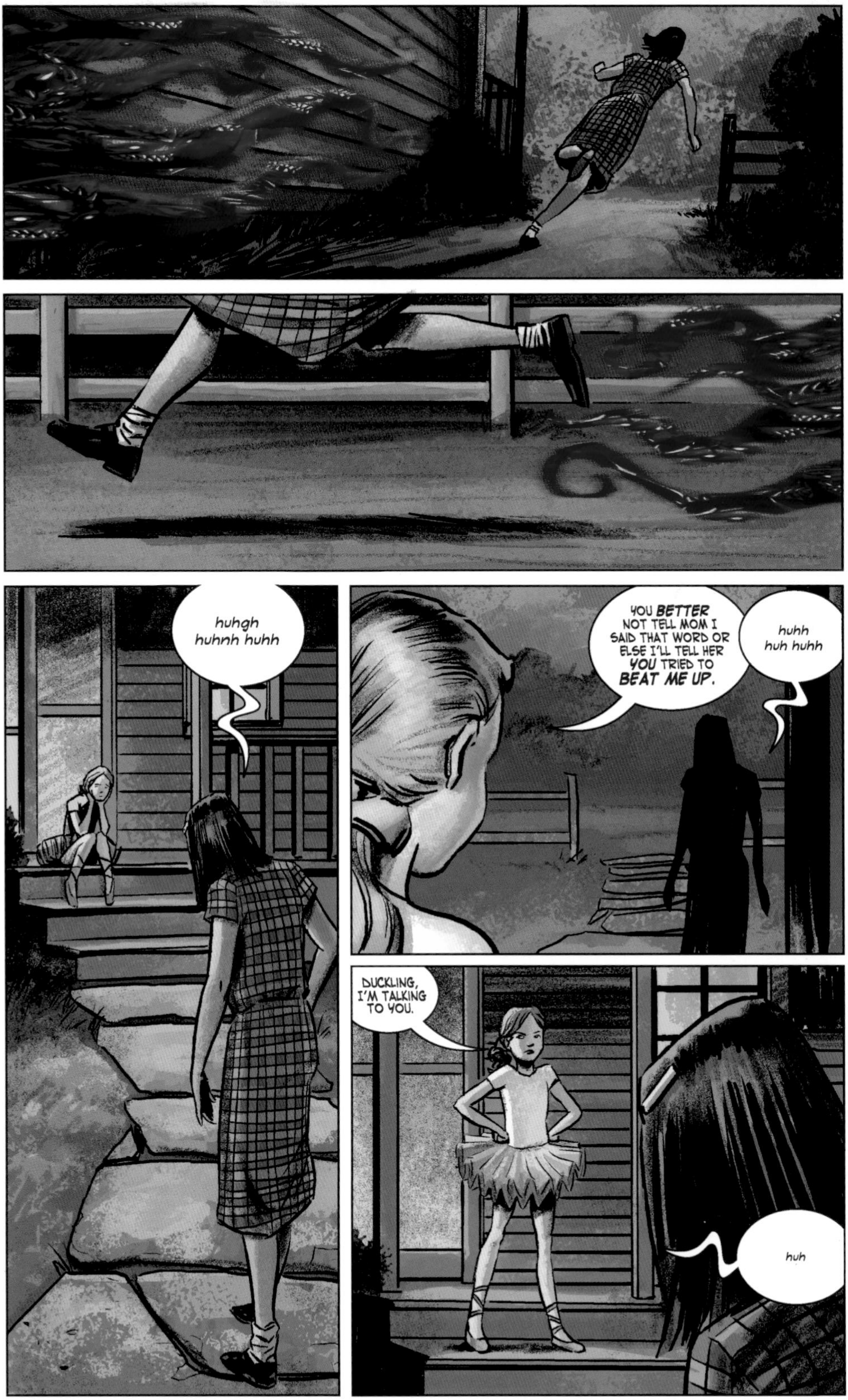
huhgh
huhnh huhh
YOU BETTER NOT TELL MOM I SAID THAT WORD OR ELSE I'LL TELL HER YOU TRIED TO BEAT ME UP.
huhh
huh huhh
DUCKLING, I'M TALKING TO YOU.
huh

OH!

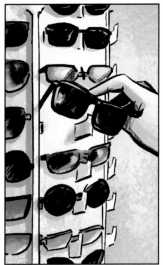

I, UH, GOTTA PAY FOR THESE TOO.

WAIT!

THP-PLASHK

‑SPHEH‑ THE *THOUGHT* OF IT... BOTHERING AN OLD WOMAN... SERVES YOU RIGHT. WANTED TO *SEEEE* SOMETHING? PEEPING ON STRANGERS? HGGGRGHHHHHMM‑...

NO, MA'AM, *PLEASE*, WHATEVER YOU DID, *PLEASE*‑‑

YOU'VE SEEN IT NOW... SEE A *LOT* MORE BEFORE LONNNNG...

IT WASN'T MY FAULT! MY *SISTER*! MY LITTLE *SPOILED‑BRAT* SISTER! SHE THREW A FIT AND RAN THROUGH YOUR YARD, SO I‑‑

OOOOOOOHHHHHHHHH...

YOUR SISTER...

A LITTLE PRINCESS IS SHE, AN AWFUL SUFFERANCE FOR SOOT‑STAINED CINDERELLA? IT'S THE *SISSSSTER* DESERVING OF MY DISCIPLINE?

PERHAPS YOU WOULD PASS IT TO HER? YES, MY *DEARRRRR*...

YOU SAW MY YOUNG *GENTLEMEN* CALLERS. SOON THEY'RE*AAAALLLLL* YOU'LL SEE.

BUT IF YOU WOULD DO THIS‑‑PUNISH THE SELFISH THING YOUR MOTHER PUSHED INTO YOUR LIFE‑‑YOU WOULD BE LIKE A DAUGHTER TO *MEEEEEEE*... TO WHOM I MIGHT INDEED PASS ON *MUCH* WISDOM...

MINE EYES HAVE SEEN THE GLORY, YES, OF GREAT AND TERRIBLE THINGS. SOON TOO WILL YOURS ‑‑THERE CAN BE NO LOOKING AWAY. A BLESSING FOR SOME. A CURSE FOR OTHERS.

GIVE THIS TO THE CHILD, MY DEAR‑‑THE *BURDEN* WILL BE ON *HER*. WHERE IT BELONGS, NOOOOOOOO?

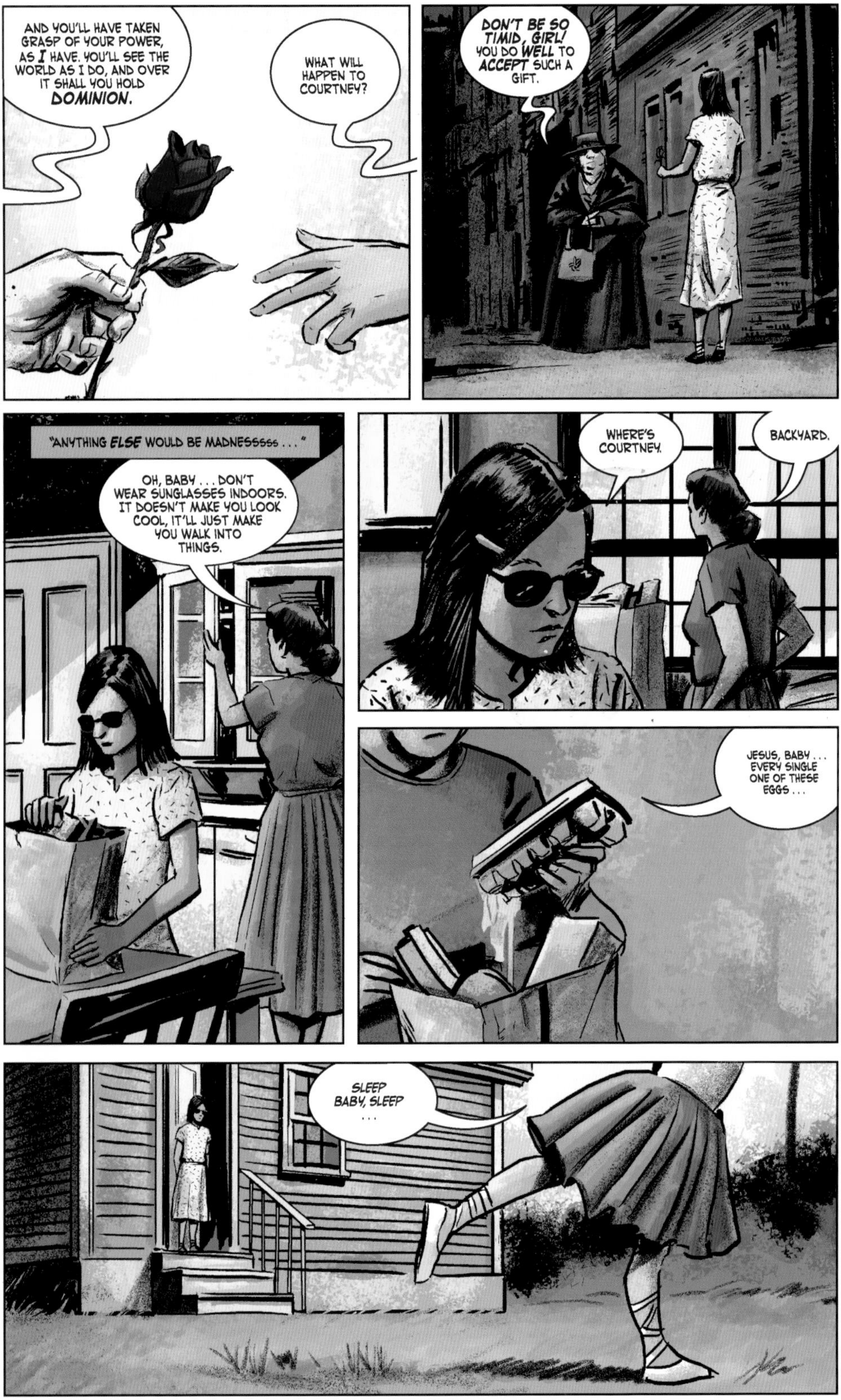
AND YOU'LL HAVE TAKEN GRASP OF YOUR POWER, AS I HAVE. YOU'LL SEE THE WORLD AS I DO, AND OVER IT SHALL YOU HOLD DOMINION.
WHAT WILL HAPPEN TO COURTNEY?
DON'T BE SO TIMID, GIRL! YOU DO WELL TO ACCEPT SUCH A GIFT.
"ANYTHING ELSE WOULD BE MADNESSSSS . . ."
OH, BABY . . . DON'T WEAR SUNGLASSES INDOORS. IT DOESN'T MAKE YOU LOOK COOL, IT'LL JUST MAKE YOU WALK INTO THINGS.
WHERE'S COURTNEY.
BACKYARD.
JESUS, BABY . . . EVERY SINGLE ONE OF THESE EGGS . . .
SLEEP BABY, SLEEP . . .

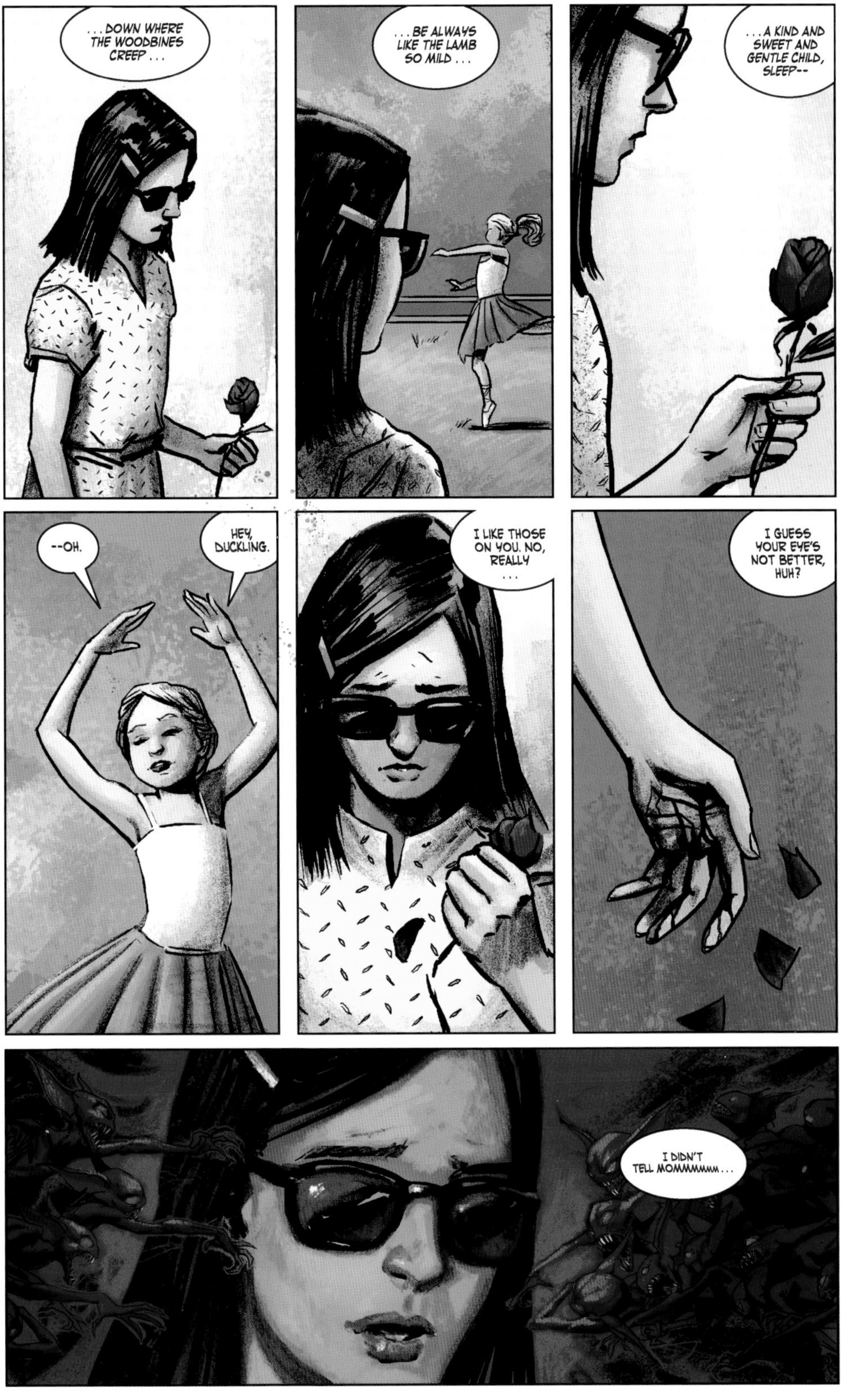

. . . DOWN WHERE THE WOODBINES CREEP . . .
. . . BE ALWAYS LIKE THE LAMB SO MILD . . .
. . . A KIND AND SWEET AND GENTLE CHILD, SLEEP--
--OH.
HEY, DUCKLING.
I LIKE THOSE ON YOU. NO, REALLY . . .
I GUESS YOUR EYE'S NOT BETTER, HUH?
I DIDN'T TELL MOMMMMMM . . .

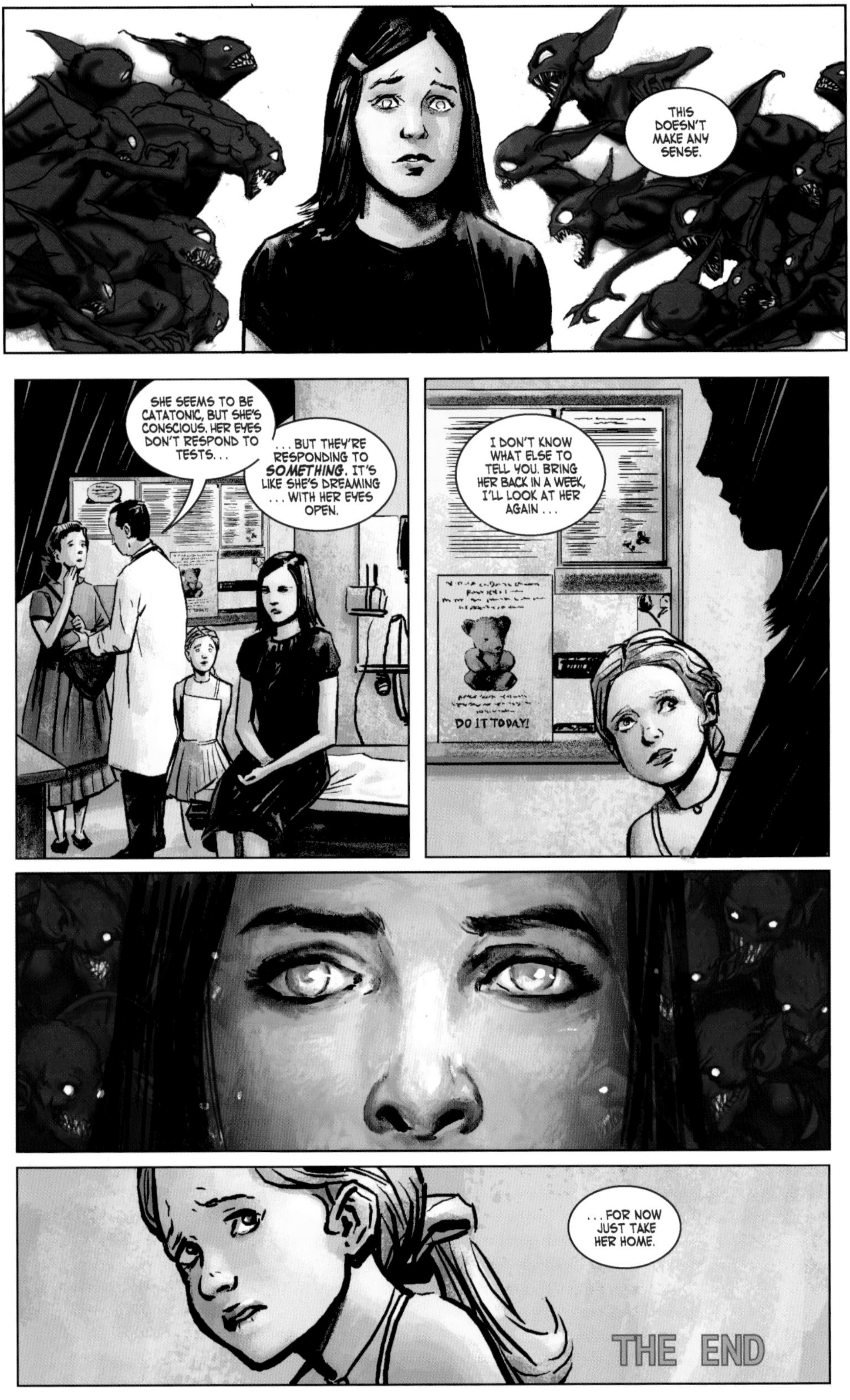

THIS DOESN'T MAKE ANY SENSE.
SHE SEEMS TO BE CATATONIC, BUT SHE'S CONSCIOUS. HER EYES DON'T RESPOND TO TESTS...
...BUT THEY'RE RESPONDING TO *SOMETHING*. IT'S LIKE SHE'S DREAMING ...WITH HER EYES OPEN.
I DON'T KNOW WHAT ELSE TO TELL YOU. BRING HER BACK IN A WEEK, I'LL LOOK AT HER AGAIN...
DO IT TODAY!
...FOR NOW JUST TAKE HER HOME.
THE END

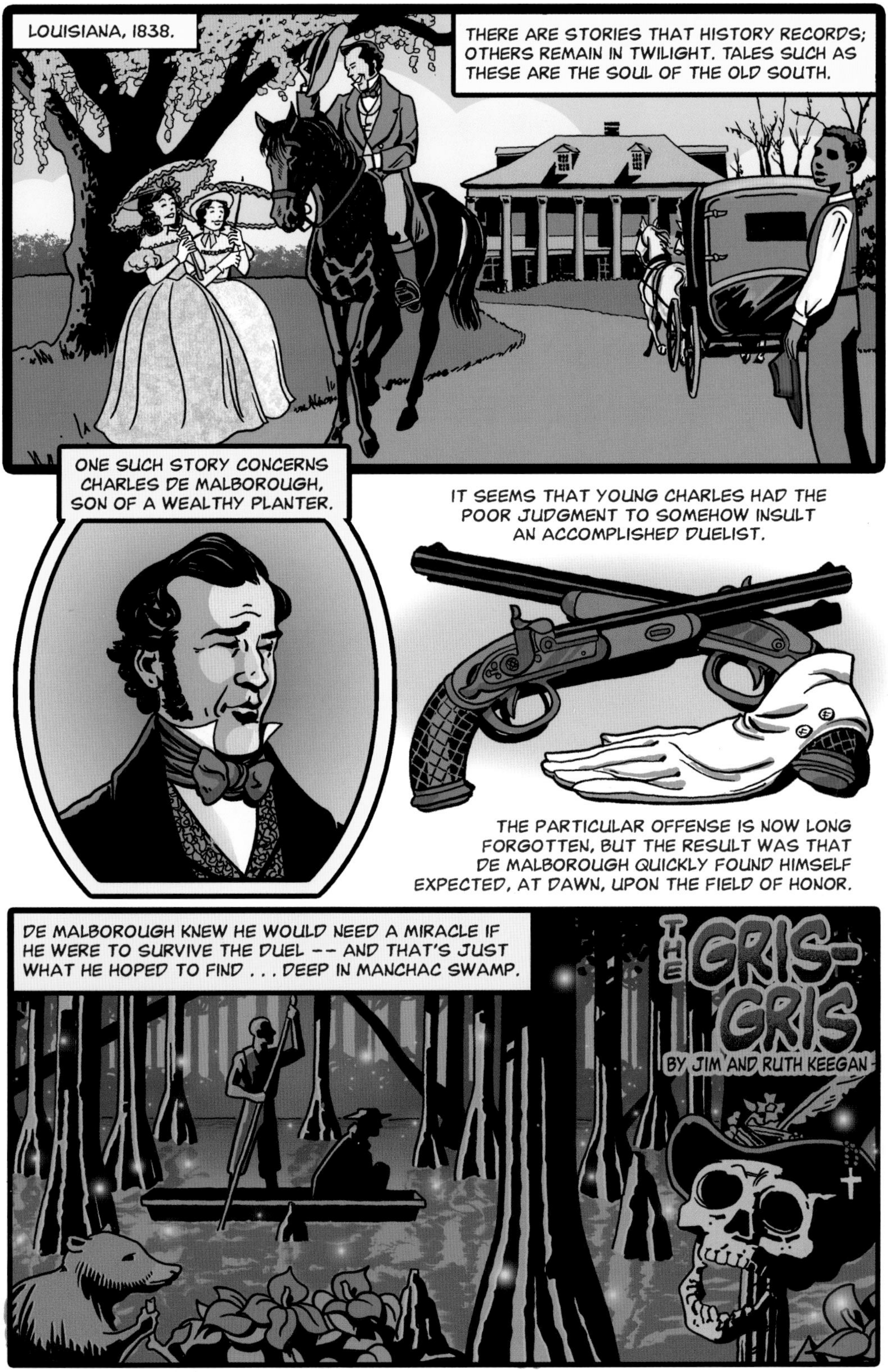
LOUISIANA, 1838.
THERE ARE STORIES THAT HISTORY RECORDS; OTHERS REMAIN IN TWILIGHT. TALES SUCH AS THESE ARE THE SOUL OF THE OLD SOUTH.
ONE SUCH STORY CONCERNS CHARLES DE MALBOROUGH, SON OF A WEALTHY PLANTER.
IT SEEMS THAT YOUNG CHARLES HAD THE POOR JUDGMENT TO SOMEHOW INSULT AN ACCOMPLISHED DUELIST.
THE PARTICULAR OFFENSE IS NOW LONG FORGOTTEN, BUT THE RESULT WAS THAT DE MALBOROUGH QUICKLY FOUND HIMSELF EXPECTED, AT DAWN, UPON THE FIELD OF HONOR.
DE MALBOROUGH KNEW HE WOULD NEED A MIRACLE IF HE WERE TO SURVIVE THE DUEL -- AND THAT'S JUST WHAT HE HOPED TO FIND . . . DEEP IN MANCHAC SWAMP.
THE GRIS-GRIS
BY JIM AND RUTH KEEGAN

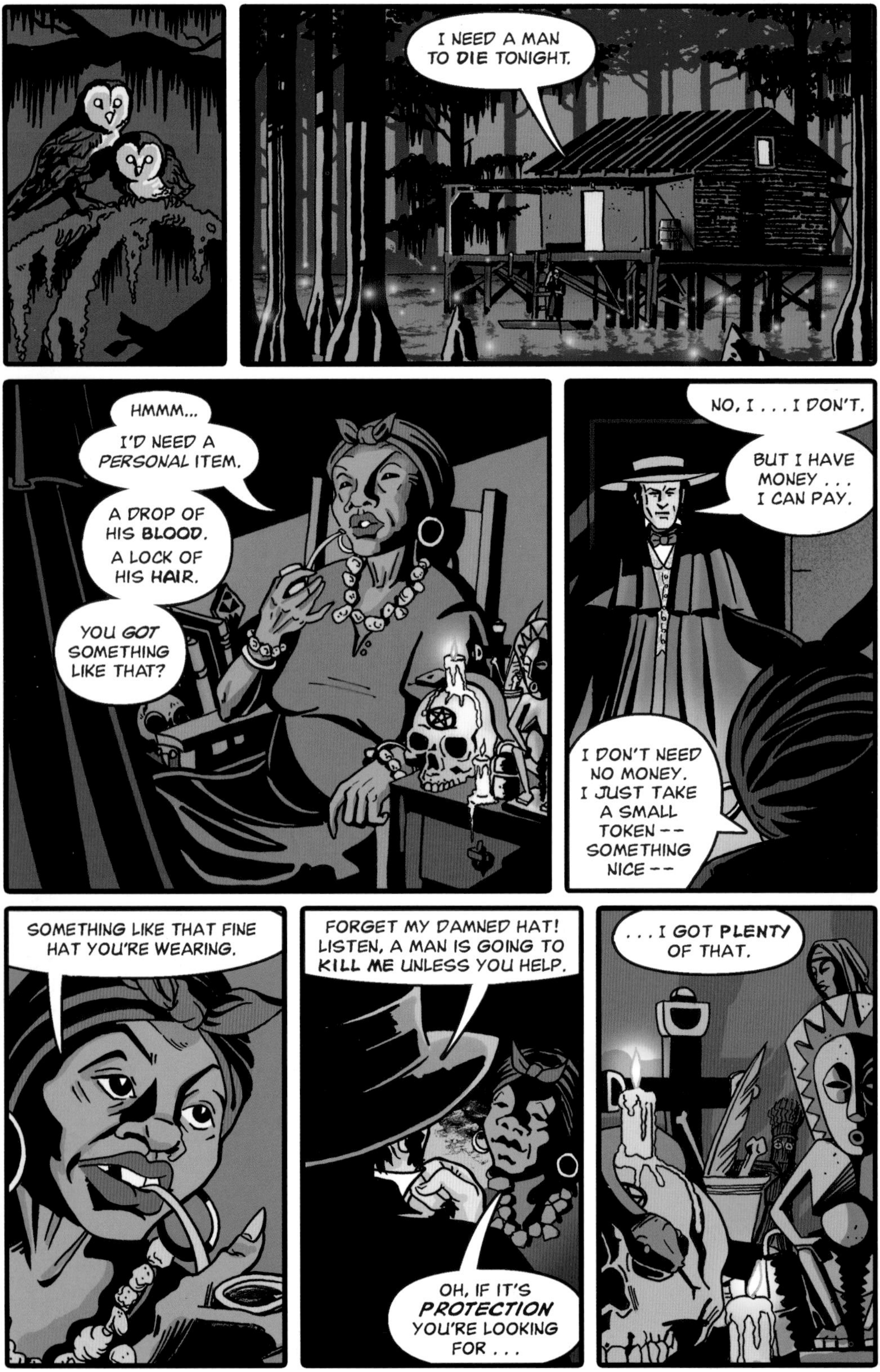

I NEED A MAN TO DIE TONIGHT.
HMMM...
I'D NEED A PERSONAL ITEM.
A DROP OF HIS BLOOD. A LOCK OF HIS HAIR.
YOU GOT SOMETHING LIKE THAT?
NO, I . . . I DON'T.
BUT I HAVE MONEY . . . I CAN PAY.
I DON'T NEED NO MONEY. I JUST TAKE A SMALL TOKEN -- SOMETHING NICE --
SOMETHING LIKE THAT FINE HAT YOU'RE WEARING.
FORGET MY DAMNED HAT! LISTEN, A MAN IS GOING TO KILL ME UNLESS YOU HELP.
OH, IF IT'S PROTECTION YOU'RE LOOKING FOR . . .
. . . I GOT PLENTY OF THAT.

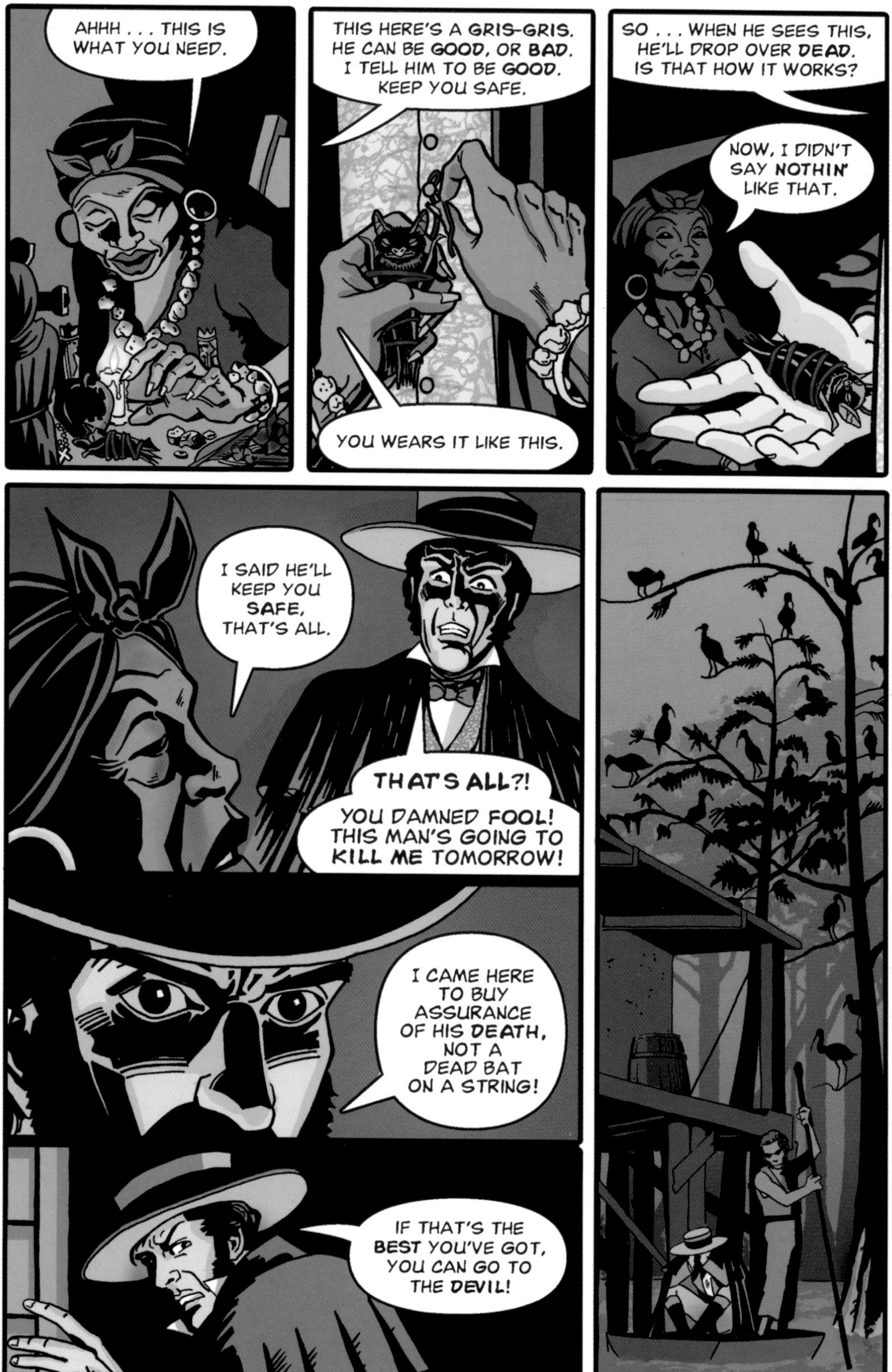
AHHH . . . THIS IS WHAT YOU NEED.
THIS HERE'S A GRIS-GRIS. HE CAN BE GOOD, OR BAD. I TELL HIM TO BE GOOD. KEEP YOU SAFE.
YOU WEARS IT LIKE THIS.
SO . . . WHEN HE SEES THIS, HE'LL DROP OVER DEAD. IS THAT HOW IT WORKS?
NOW, I DIDN'T SAY NOTHIN' LIKE THAT.
I SAID HE'LL KEEP YOU SAFE, THAT'S ALL.
THAT'S ALL?!
YOU DAMNED FOOL! THIS MAN'S GOING TO KILL ME TOMORROW!
I CAME HERE TO BUY ASSURANCE OF HIS DEATH, NOT A DEAD BAT ON A STRING!
IF THAT'S THE BEST YOU'VE GOT, YOU CAN GO TO THE DEVIL!

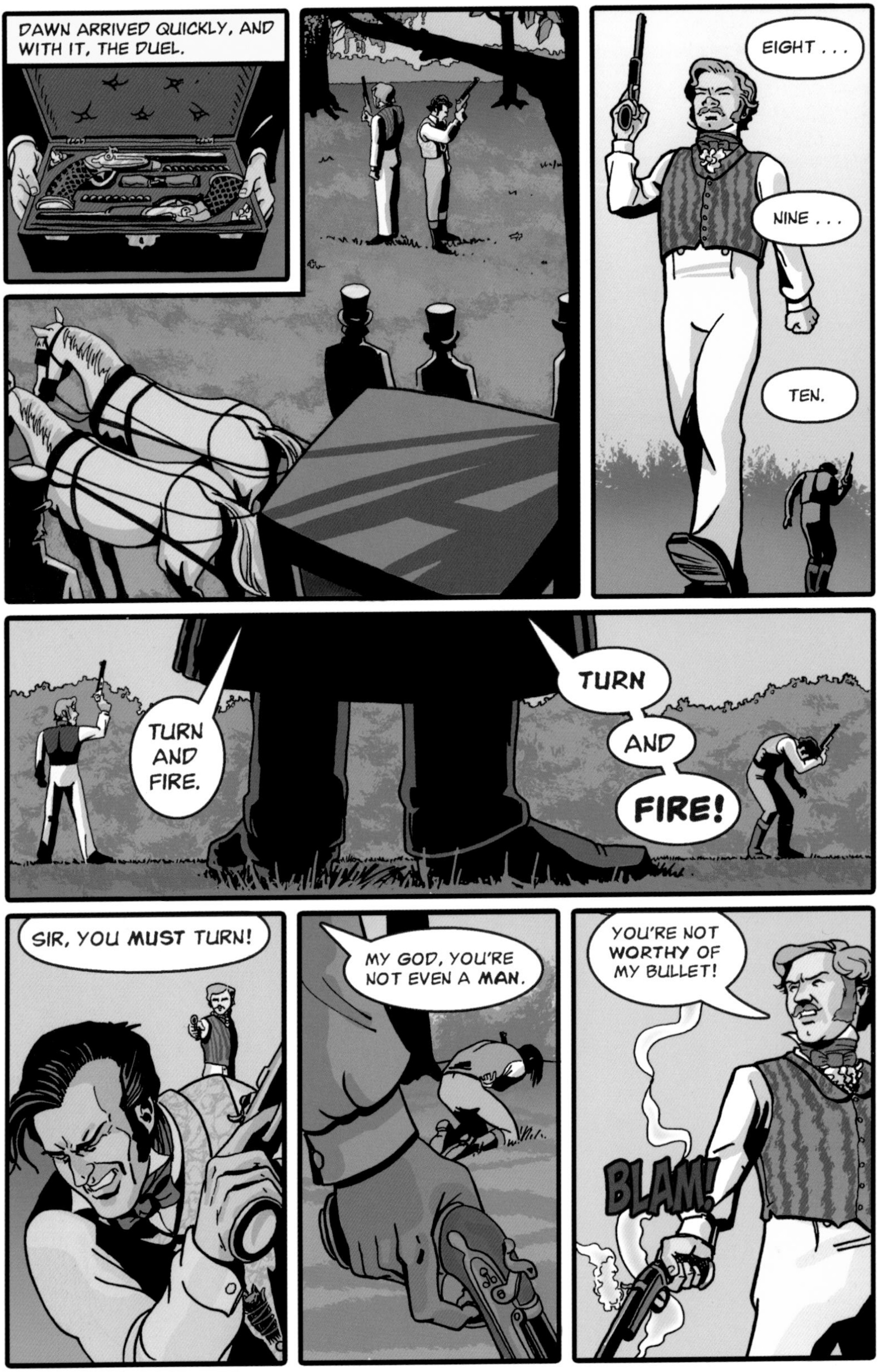
DAWN ARRIVED QUICKLY, AND WITH IT, THE DUEL.
EIGHT . . .
NINE . . .
TEN.
TURN AND FIRE.
TURN
AND
FIRE!
SIR, YOU MUST TURN!
MY GOD, YOU'RE NOT EVEN A MAN.
YOU'RE NOT WORTHY OF MY BULLET!
BLAM!

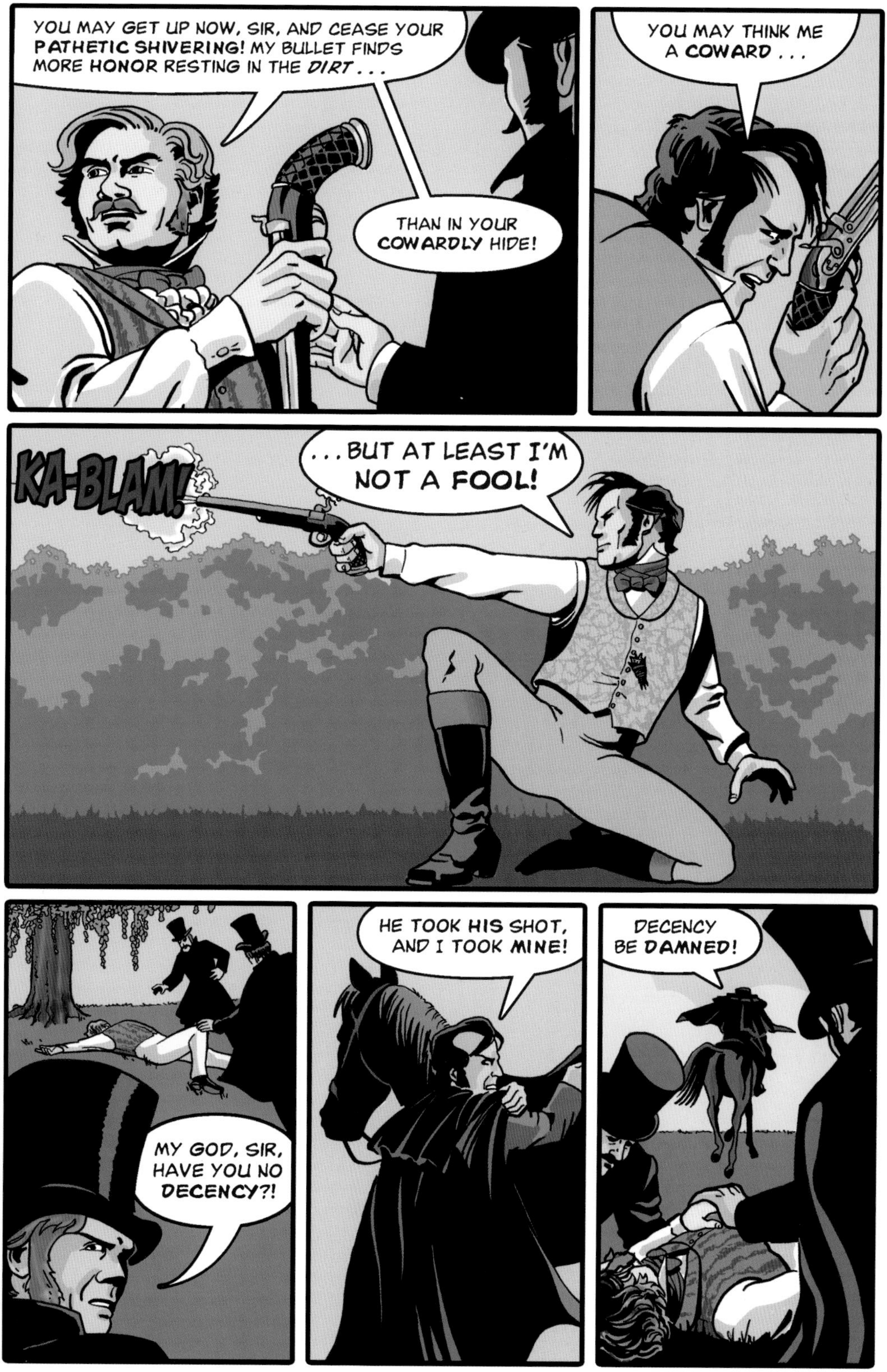
YOU MAY GET UP NOW, SIR, AND CEASE YOUR PATHETIC SHIVERING! MY BULLET FINDS MORE HONOR RESTING IN THE DIRT . . .
THAN IN YOUR COWARDLY HIDE!
YOU MAY THINK ME A COWARD . . .
KA-BLAM!
. . . BUT AT LEAST I'M NOT A FOOL!
MY GOD, SIR, HAVE YOU NO DECENCY?!
HE TOOK HIS SHOT, AND I TOOK MINE!
DECENCY BE DAMNED!

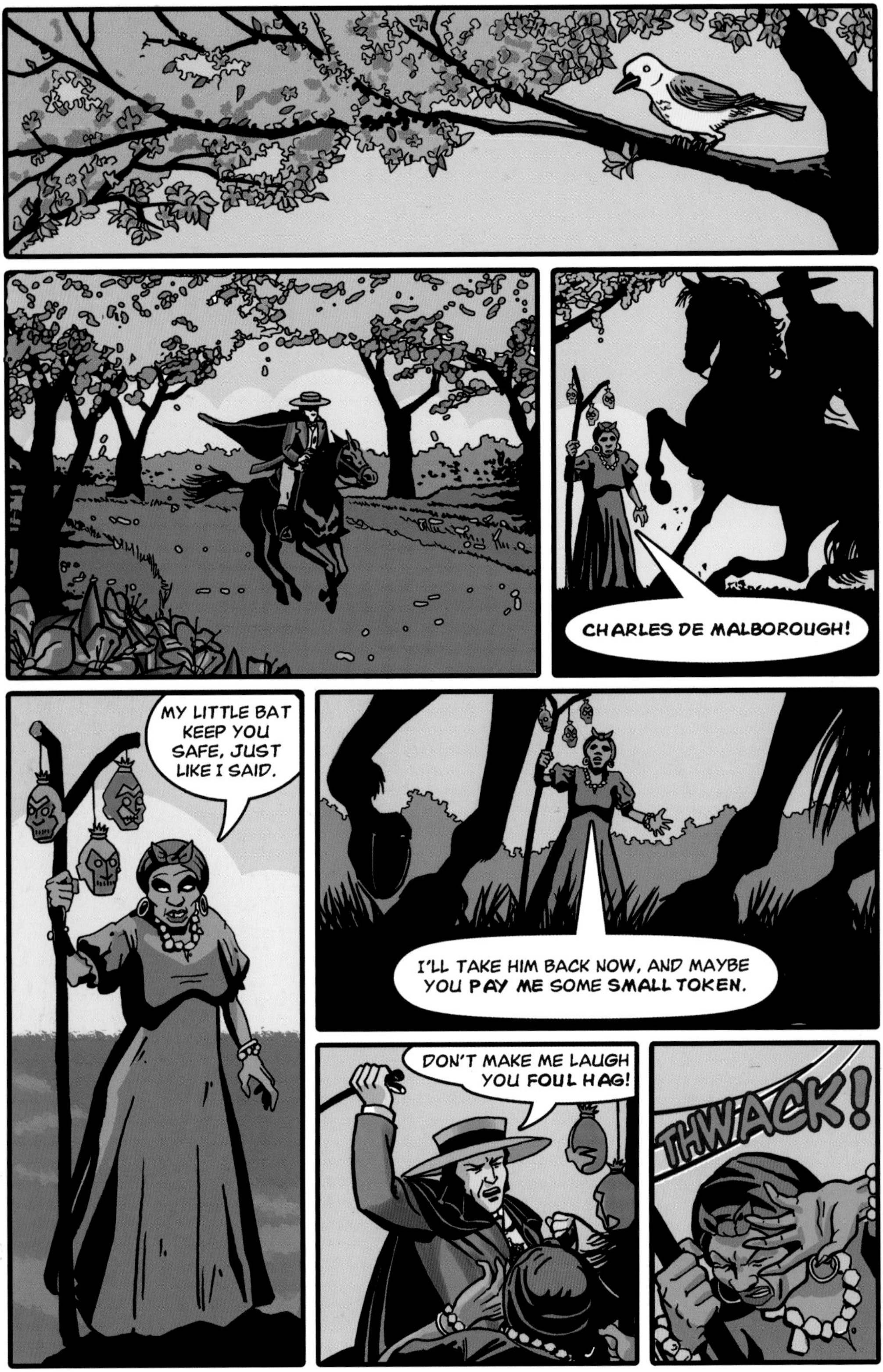
CHARLES DE MALBOROUGH!
MY LITTLE BAT KEEP YOU SAFE, JUST LIKE I SAID.
I'LL TAKE HIM BACK NOW, AND MAYBE YOU PAY ME SOME SMALL TOKEN.
DON'T MAKE ME LAUGH YOU FOUL HAG!
THWACK!

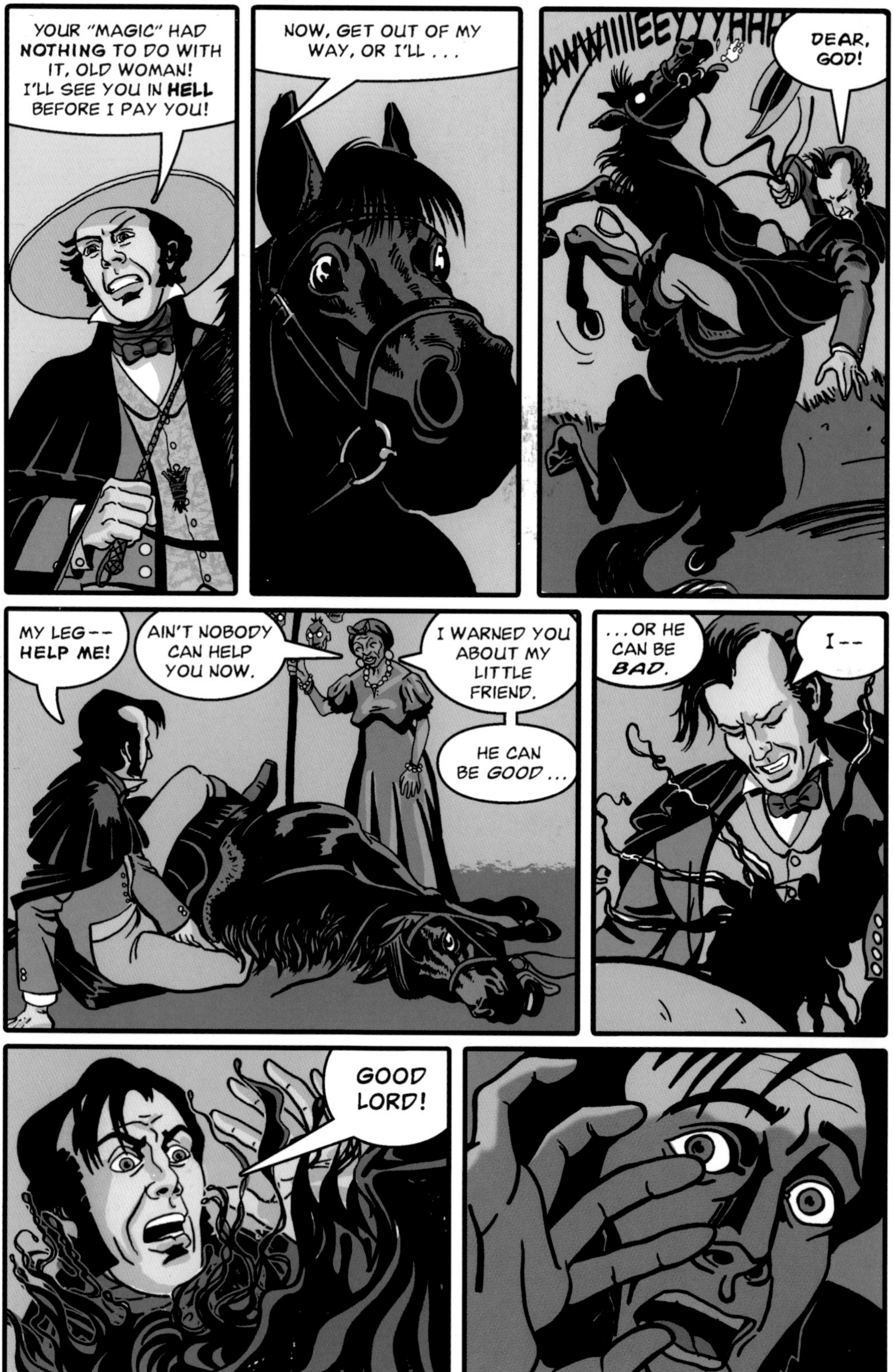
YOUR "MAGIC" HAD **NOTHING** TO DO WITH IT, OLD WOMAN! I'LL SEE YOU IN **HELL** BEFORE I PAY YOU!
NOW, GET OUT OF MY WAY, OR I'LL . . .
WWWIIIIEEYYYHH
DEAR, GOD!
MY LEG-- **HELP ME!**
AIN'T NOBODY CAN HELP YOU NOW.
I WARNED YOU ABOUT MY LITTLE FRIEND.
HE CAN BE *GOOD* . . .
. . . OR HE CAN BE ***BAD***.
I--
GOOD LORD!

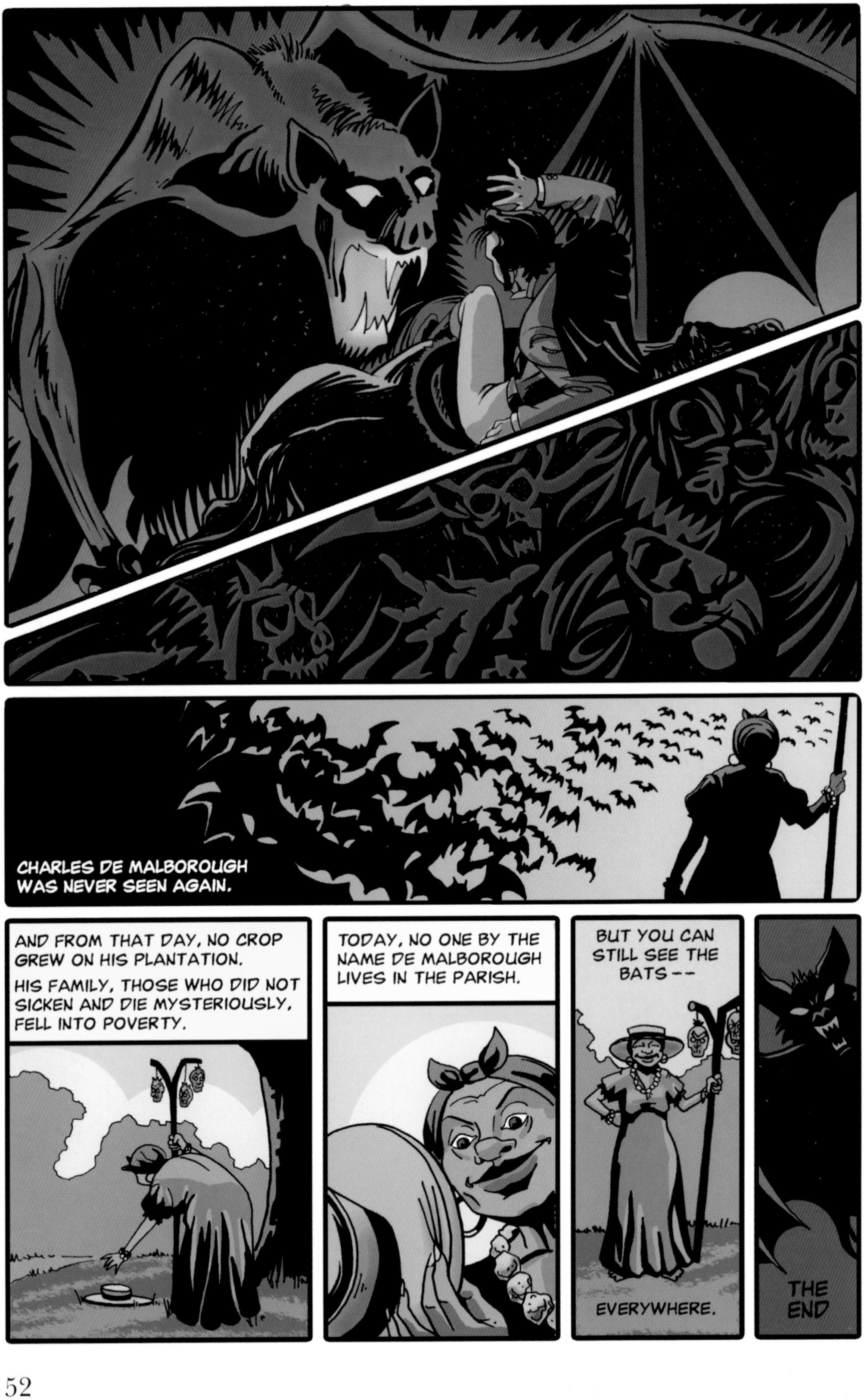
CHARLES DE MALBOROUGH WAS NEVER SEEN AGAIN.
AND FROM THAT DAY, NO CROP GREW ON HIS PLANTATION.
HIS FAMILY, THOSE WHO DID NOT SICKEN AND DIE MYSTERIOUSLY, FELL INTO POVERTY.
TODAY, NO ONE BY THE NAME DE MALBOROUGH LIVES IN THE PARISH.
BUT YOU CAN STILL SEE THE BATS --
EVERYWHERE.
THE END

Golden Calf Blues

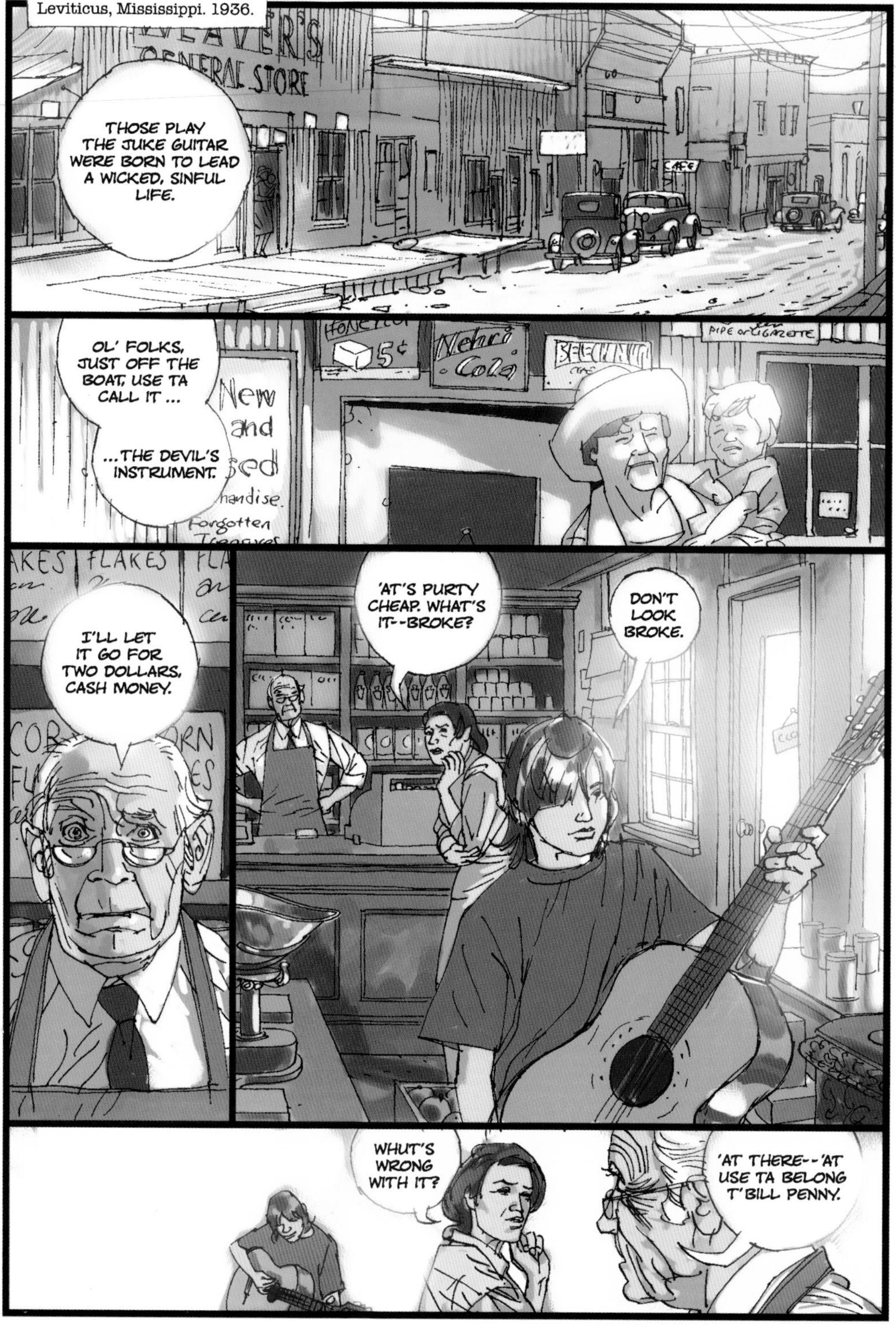
Leviticus, Mississippi. 1936.
WEAVER'S GENERAL STORE
THOSE PLAY THE JUKE GUITAR WERE BORN TO LEAD A WICKED, SINFUL LIFE.
CAFE
OL' FOLKS, JUST OFF THE BOAT, USE TA CALL IT ...
...THE DEVIL'S INSTRUMENT.
5¢
Nehi Cola
PIPE or CIGARETTE
New and Used
Forgotten
I'LL LET IT GO FOR TWO DOLLARS, CASH MONEY.
'AT'S PURTY CHEAP. WHAT'S IT--BROKE?
DON'T LOOK BROKE.
WHUT'S WRONG WITH IT?
'AT THERE--'AT USE TA BELONG T' BILL PENNY.

By Mark Ricketts & Sean Phillips

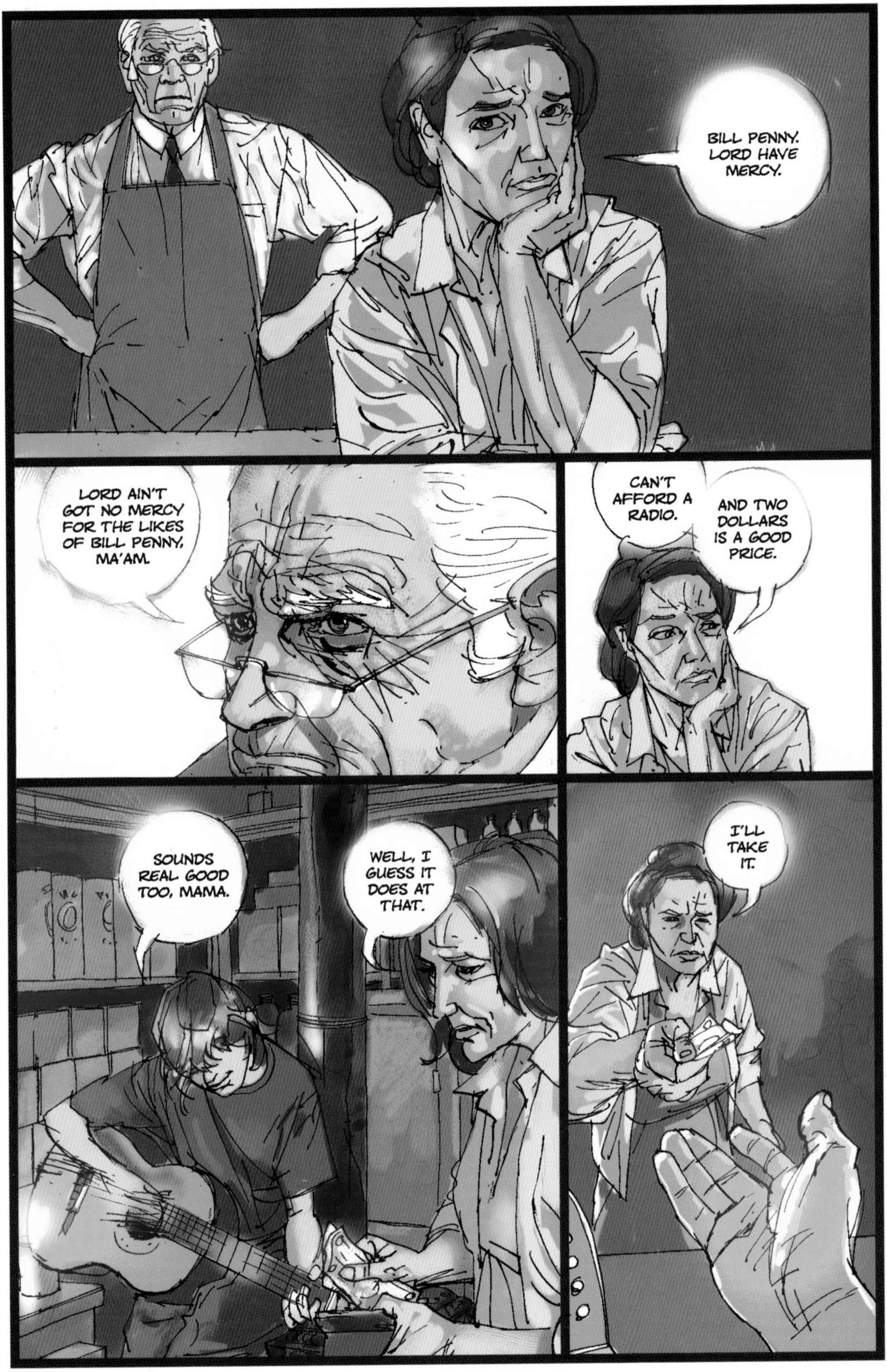
BILL PENNY. LORD HAVE MERCY.
LORD AIN'T GOT NO MERCY FOR THE LIKES OF BILL PENNY, MA'AM.
CAN'T AFFORD A RADIO.
AND TWO DOLLARS IS A GOOD PRICE.
SOUNDS REAL GOOD TOO, MAMA.
WELL, I GUESS IT DOES AT THAT.
I'LL TAKE IT.

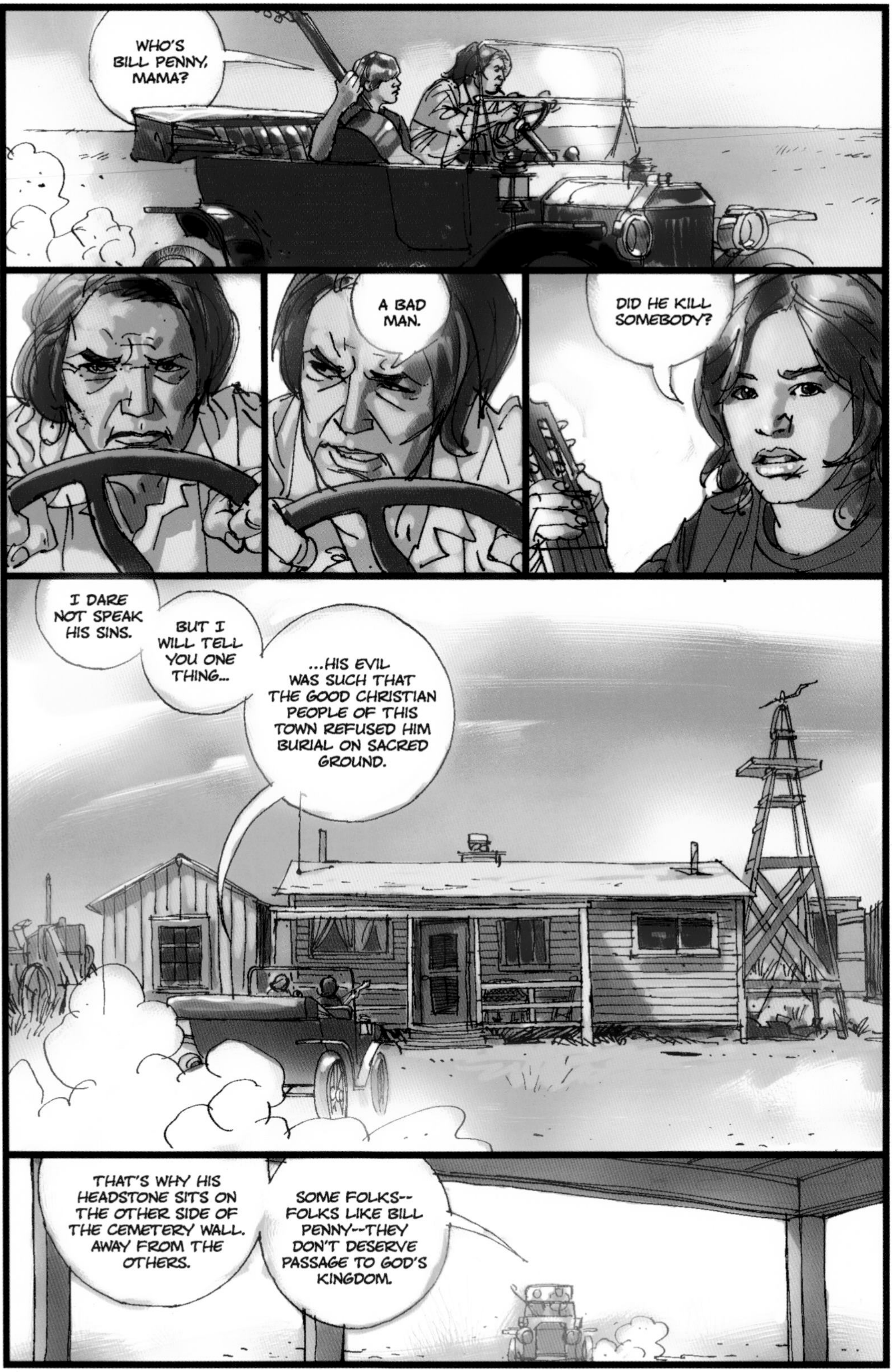
WHO'S BILL PENNY, MAMA?
A BAD MAN.
DID HE KILL SOMEBODY?
I DARE NOT SPEAK HIS SINS.
BUT I WILL TELL YOU ONE THING...
...HIS EVIL WAS SUCH THAT THE GOOD CHRISTIAN PEOPLE OF THIS TOWN REFUSED HIM BURIAL ON SACRED GROUND.
THAT'S WHY HIS HEADSTONE SITS ON THE OTHER SIDE OF THE CEMETERY WALL. AWAY FROM THE OTHERS.
SOME FOLKS-- FOLKS LIKE BILL PENNY--THEY DON'T DESERVE PASSAGE TO GOD'S KINGDOM.

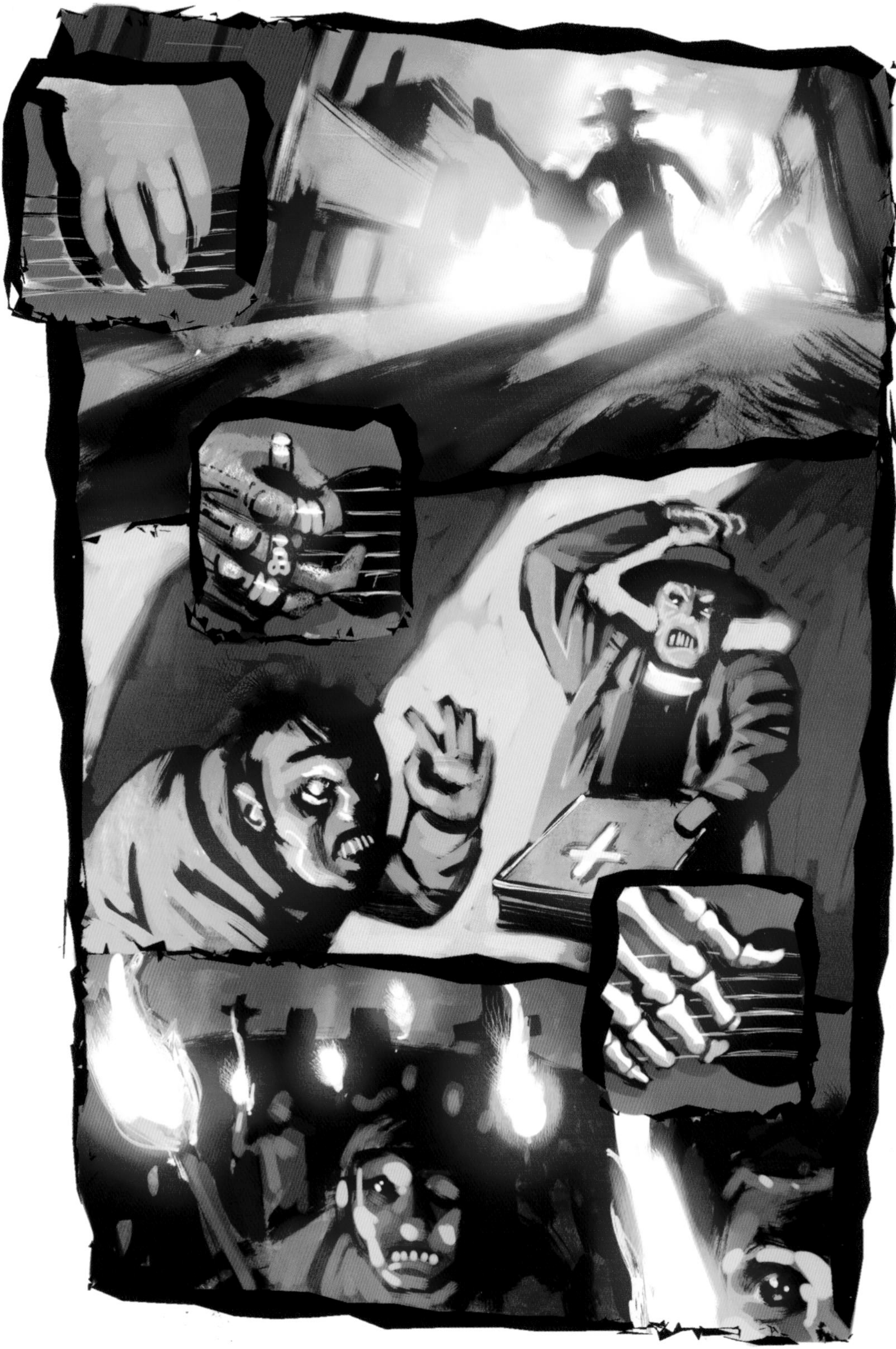

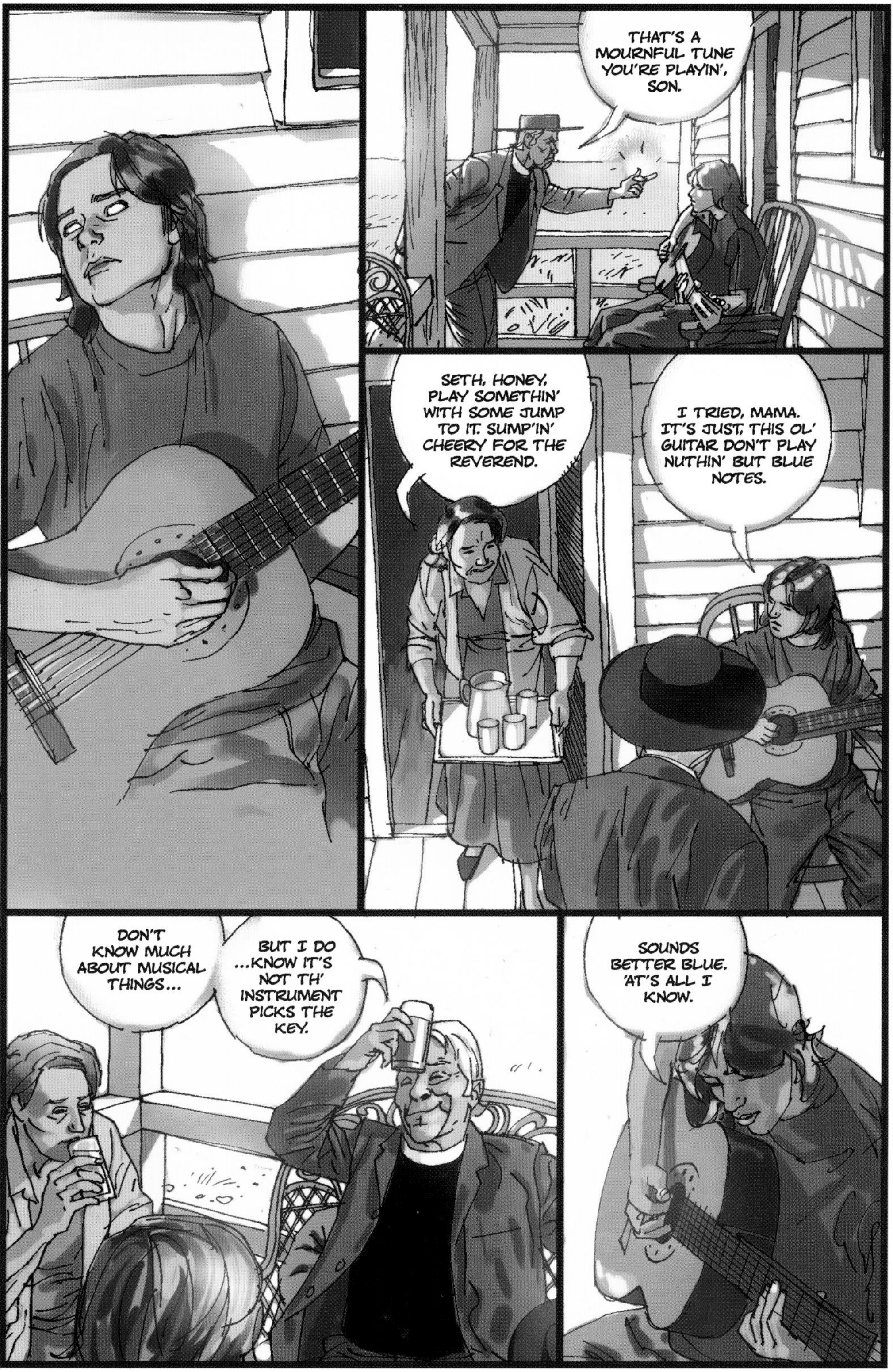
THAT'S A MOURNFUL TUNE YOU'RE PLAYIN', SON.
SETH, HONEY, PLAY SOMETHIN' WITH SOME JUMP TO IT. SUMP'IN' CHEERY FOR THE REVEREND.
I TRIED, MAMA. IT'S JUST, THIS OL' GUITAR DON'T PLAY NUTHIN' BUT BLUE NOTES.
DON'T KNOW MUCH ABOUT MUSICAL THINGS...
BUT I DO ...KNOW IT'S NOT TH' INSTRUMENT PICKS THE KEY.
SOUNDS BETTER BLUE. 'AT'S ALL I KNOW.

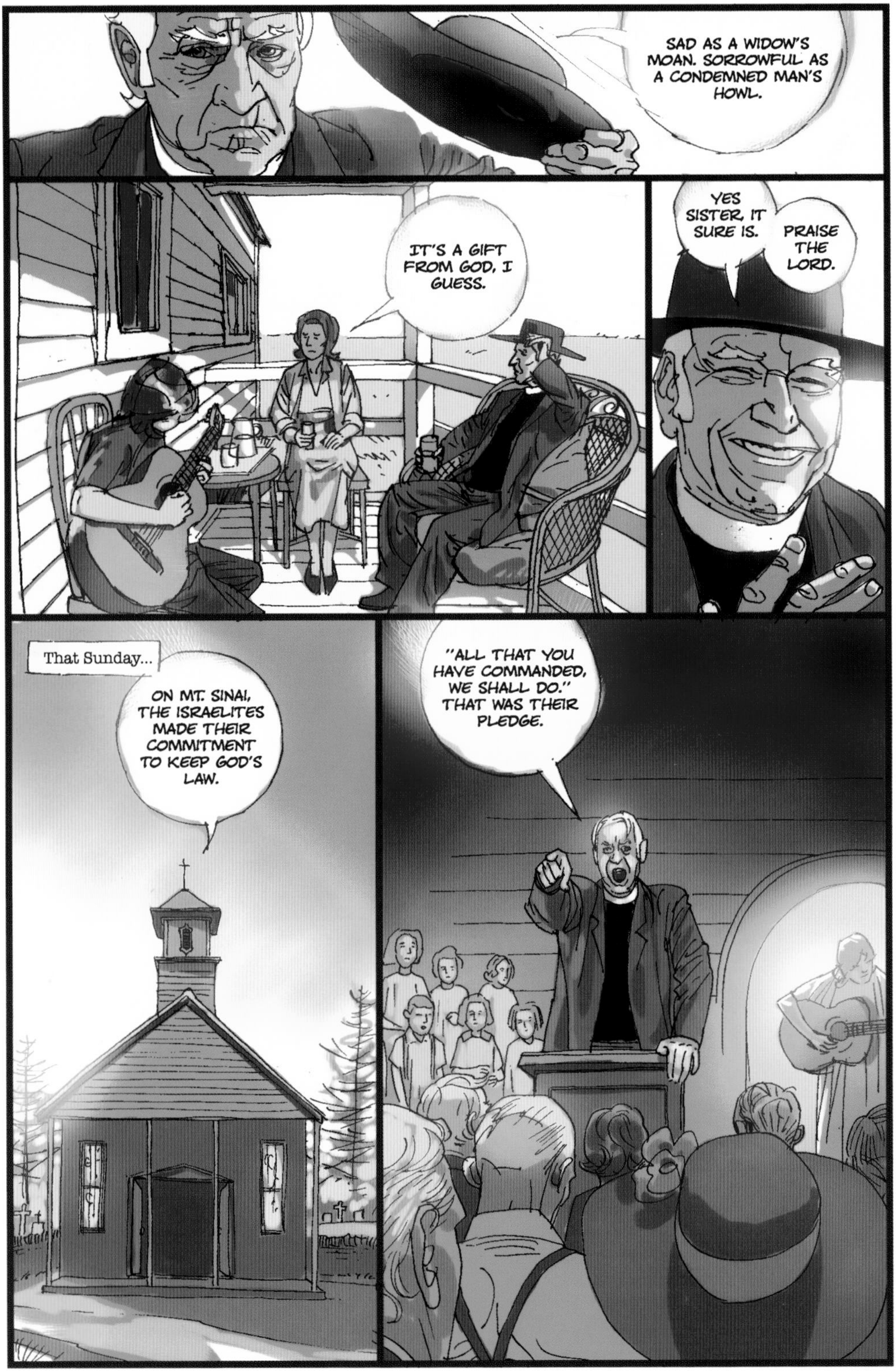
SAD AS A WIDOW'S MOAN. SORROWFUL AS A CONDEMNED MAN'S HOWL.
IT'S A GIFT FROM GOD, I GUESS.
YES SISTER, IT SURE IS.
PRAISE THE LORD.
That Sunday...
ON MT. SINAI, THE ISRAELITES MADE THEIR COMMITMENT TO KEEP GOD'S LAW.
"ALL THAT YOU HAVE COMMANDED, WE SHALL DO." THAT WAS THEIR PLEDGE.

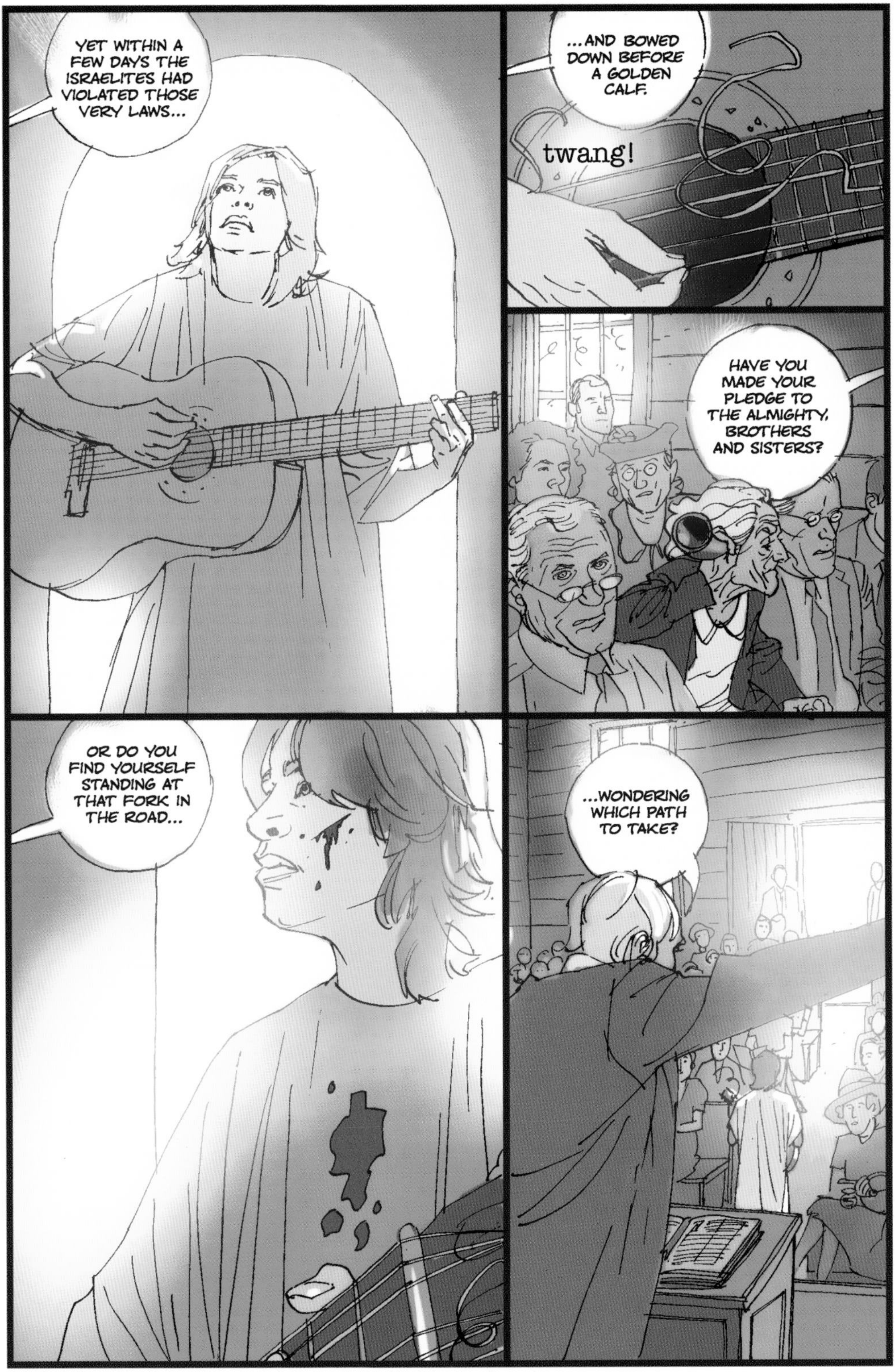
YET WITHIN A FEW DAYS THE ISRAELITES HAD VIOLATED THOSE VERY LAWS...
...AND BOWED DOWN BEFORE A GOLDEN CALF.
twang!
HAVE YOU MADE YOUR PLEDGE TO THE ALMIGHTY, BROTHERS AND SISTERS?
OR DO YOU FIND YOURSELF STANDING AT THAT FORK IN THE ROAD...
...WONDERING WHICH PATH TO TAKE?

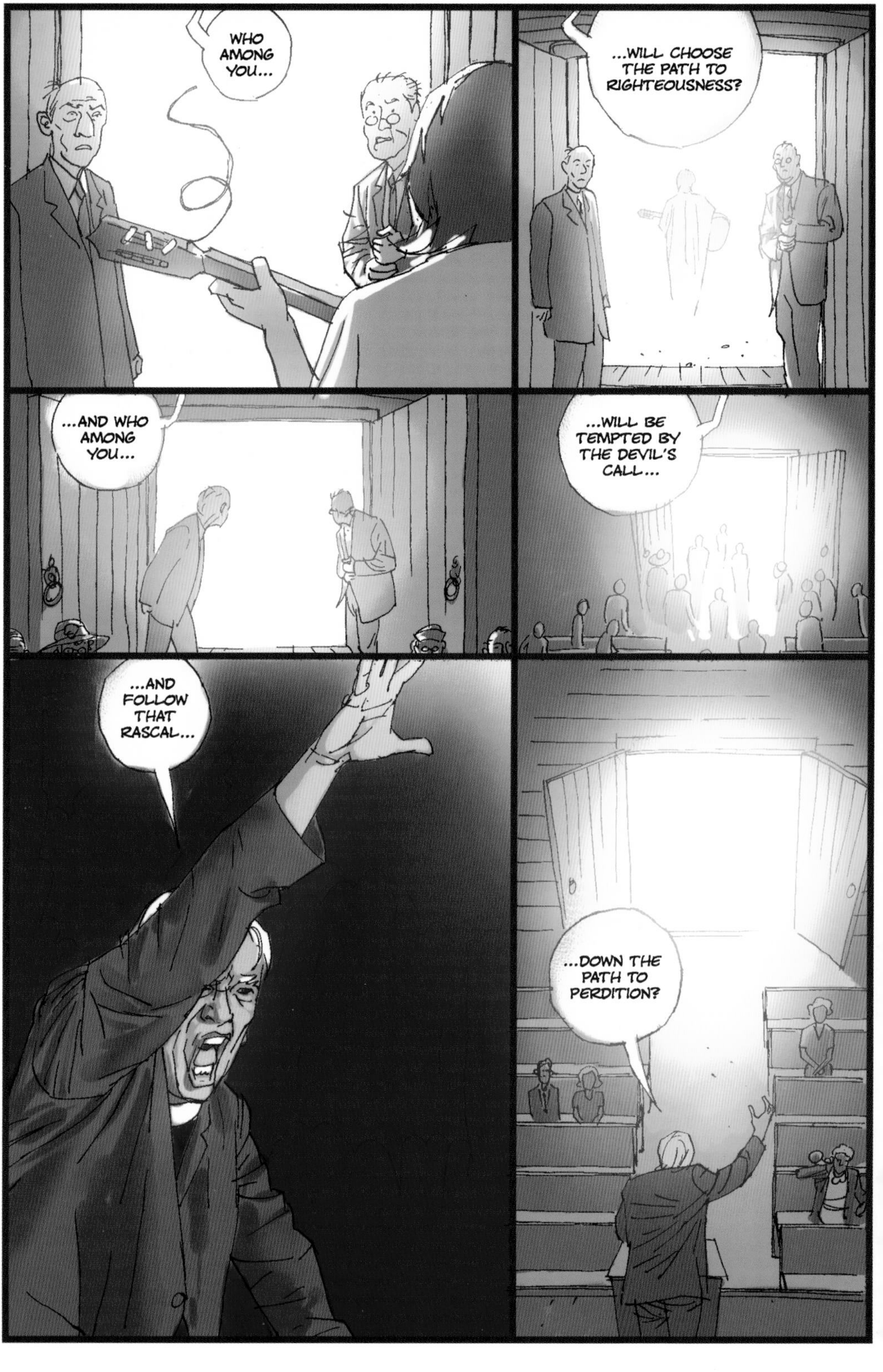
WHO AMONG YOU...
...WILL CHOOSE THE PATH TO RIGHTEOUSNESS?
...AND WHO AMONG YOU...
...WILL BE TEMPTED BY THE DEVIL'S CALL...
...AND FOLLOW THAT RASCAL...
...DOWN THE PATH TO PERDITION?

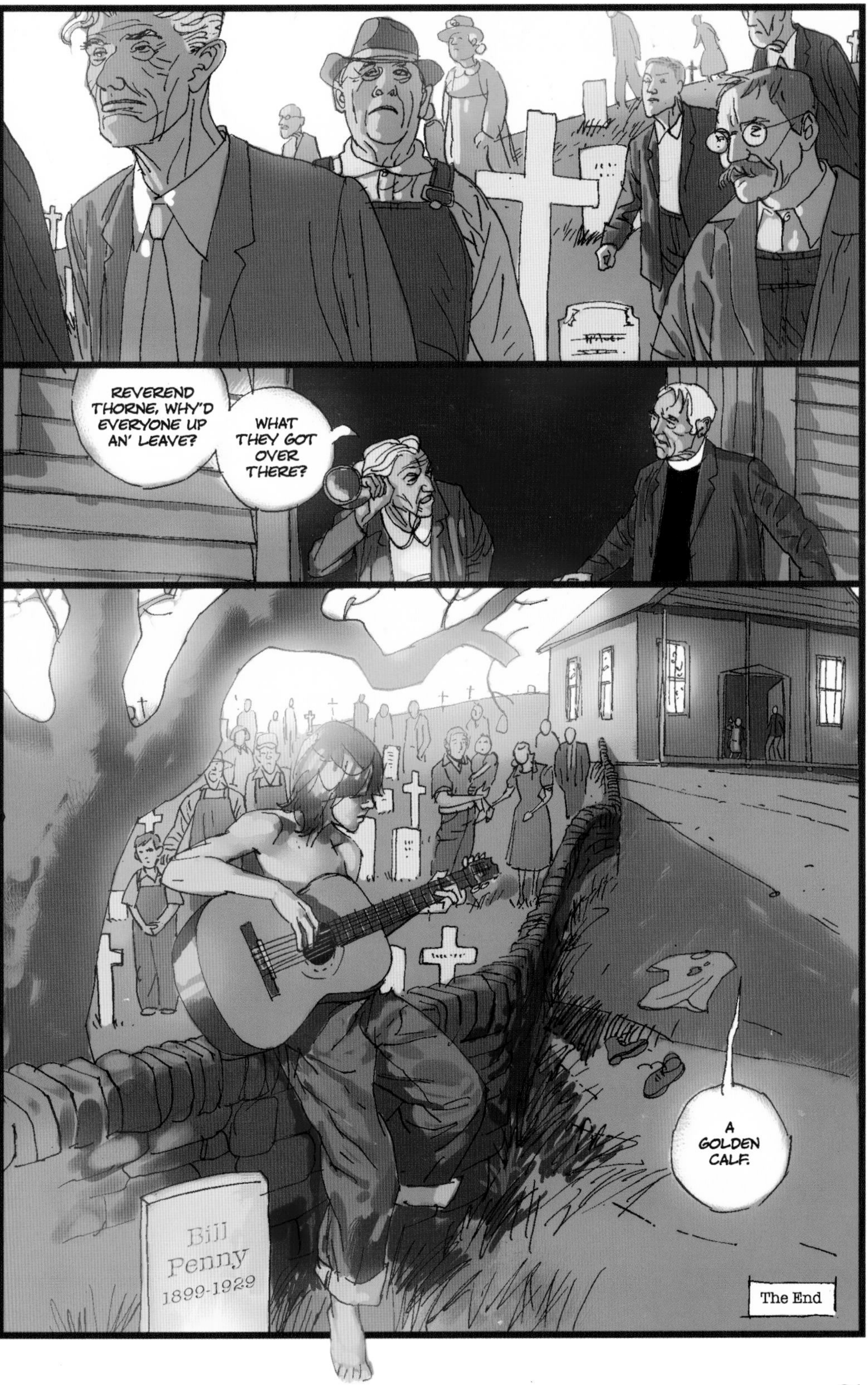
REVEREND THORNE, WHY'D EVERYONE UP AN' LEAVE?
WHAT THEY GOT OVER THERE?
A GOLDEN CALF.
Bill Penny 1899-1929
The End

The Truth about Witchcraft

An interview with Wiccan High Priestess
PHYLLIS CUROTT

by SCOTT ALLIE

Photo © Bruce Fields

*H*Ps. *Phyllis Curott, J.D., was named alongside Hilary Clinton as one of the Ten Gutsiest Women of the Year by* Jane Magazine *and described by* New York Magazine *as one of NYC's most intellectually cutting-edge speakers. As an attorney, she has successfully won the right of Wiccan clergy to perform marriages in New York City, and has been a pro bono consultant on numerous religious liberties cases. She was a member of the United Nations' Committee on the Status of Women, and is the Wiccan representative to the Harvard University's Consultation on Religious Discrimination and Accommodation. She serves on the Association for Union Democracy, opposing corruption in trade unions. She began her legal career as the Legal Director for PROD/Teamsters for a Democratic Union, fighting organized crime within the Teamsters union. Ms. Curott studied filmmaking at NYU, producing several independent features, including* New Year's Day, *which competed in the Venice Film Festival, as well as several short films screened at the Cannes and Sundance Film Festivals. She received her B.A. in philosophy from Brown University, and her Juris Doctor from New York University School of Law. She continues to practice law in New York City and is at work on her third book.*

ALLIE: How did a New York lawyer become involved in Witchcraft?

CUROTT: It began with a summoning from a presence I call the daemon. Socrates talked about his daemon; a divine figure that lives within you, like a muse. During my last year in law school, he laid down a trail of breadcrumbs in the form of synchronicities. I think these things happen to almost everyone. The difference was that I was very receptive, because there was an objective component. I'm a rationalist. I needed proof, and the universe kept proving itself. Pan piped and I followed. At the time you couldn't find Witchcraft. It was extremely difficult to pry that door open. And it was flung open for me.

Did being a philosophy student at Brown help open the door?

No, my specialty was ethics and political philosophy. I was very pragmatic. And I wasn't raised in a religious household. When I asked my parents, "What religion are we?" they said, "You are half Viking and half Maccabee, and when you grow up you can look for yourself as to whether God exists." I never intended to do that, but they were looking for me. And it wasn't just God. It was the Goddess, and something beyond gender. The door between the worlds opened. It was hardly where I expected to find myself, but I was sent a sign I couldn't argue with. I'd had a repeating dream of a woman. She was seated and bare breasted, wearing a triangular crown. At her throat she had a star like a little blazing light, and a book in her hand. The star would flare and the dream would go white. Then my daemon led me into a friendship with a woman managing a rock band—and she was a Witch. She was great, so I decided to ignore that particular idiosyncrasy. One day she took me to have my cards read at the Magical Child, an occult bookstore in New York. The reading was astonishing, and I was invited to this coven. I thanked the priestess and left, and had no intention of going back. But my friend said, "It's almost impossible to get into a coven. You shouldn't blow it off." I wasn't sure. But a few days later I went to the Metropolitan Museum of Art, a very powerful, sacred space for me. I wandered into a new section, a garden filled with statuary, and right in front of me was a statue of the woman in my dream. Precisely. The room bleached out. I got lightheaded. I spent the whole afternoon staring at her. She was called The Libyan Sibyl. I went home and pulled out my dictionary and looked up the word *sibyl*. It said, "An ancient prophetess, a Witch." The next week I went back. There were about seventy-five women. Every week I was invited to come back as they whittled down that seventy-five to eight women, who became the Mother Grove of the Minoan tradition. At first it all seemed preposterous to me—real mumbo jumbo, but I wanted that quality of magic that had come to me, so I stayed.

In your second book, Witchcrafting, *you use the words* Wicca *and* Witch *interchangeably. Are you dismissing other magical practices?*

No. Wicca is a specific method of practicing within the broader movement of Witchcraft. Almost twenty years ago, the people who first went public in the United States, like Margot Adler and myself, used the term *Wicca* because that was our background. The word was used synonymously with *Witchcraft* by the media and the early movement, although it blurs distinctions. Mainstream media isn't interested in the distinctions the way we are. Some of us practice Stregheria, or Asatru—there's a long list now. The movement has become more diverse in the various ethnic traditions. I use the term *Wicca* when I deal with mainstream culture because I want people to be able to practice this religion in peace and in freedom. Every time you say *Witchcraft*, the person listening is seeing and hearing through the filter of this toxic stereotype. Using the word *Wicca* makes it easier for mainstream culture to see what this is really about. Even if the practices never make their way into mainstream culture, the core values of this spirituality are critical to the survival of the species and the planet. That's my priority. I don't like labels—they limit engagement rather than expanding it.

You talk about a process of un-naming when dealing with the natural world. Is that the same thing?

One of the things I do is look at the influences on our beliefs and practices. This is the rebirth of an ancient religion, but it's also very modern. We are creating it every time we do something. It is very personal, innovative, and creative. There are influences from ceremonial traditions which unfortunately carry biblical, patriarchal perspectives. The biblical model views God as transcendent, not present in the world. The power's out *there* somewhere. But the core experience in Witchcraft is that the divine is in us and the world and is the source of magic. But a lot of our language and practices are the opposite. One of the best examples is the ceremonial notion that by naming something you have power over it. It's a cognitive principle—if you can identify something, you are empowered. That is also a very profound magical principle. In the Bible, God and man name things; that gives them power over what's named. But when we tell ourselves we control something, we distance ourselves from it. We establish a position of power over what we've named, instead of opening ourselves to learning from it. My work is not about the projection of will, which is the old ceremonial model of magic, but about opening yourself to the divine, letting it transform and teach you. Instead of naming, like, *Oak tree*, you pay attention to it, and describe it without that term: home for birds, maker of oxygen, giver of life. And you begin to recognize connections. That's what a Witch is. Someone who pays attention to the divine. When you un-name, you engage the living divinity of the natural world. Instead of naming and having power *over*, it's un-naming and opening yourself to the power *of*.

Did Gerald Gardner create Wicca?

Without him, contemporary Wicca would not exist. Something would exist, but this movement would not. He was a link in a fascinating chain of influences and made important contributions and brought it to the public eye. For me Wicca is a dynamic spirituality—it's something we are all creating everytime we practice. I think Uncle Gerry would approve.

Gardner worked with Aleister Crowley, and Crowley died in 1947. When did Gardner popularize Wicca?

In the early fifties, when the Witchcraft laws were repealed in England. His books were published in England in the fifties, and he was interviewed on radio and in newspapers. His motivation was to keep the religion from dying out, and he did his job, far better than I think he expected.

He created the initiatory part of Wicca, right?

Well, he borrowed from various sources to create certain rituals. But there were initiations going back to Eleusis. In all indigenous religions there is an initiation, a death and rebirth experience. He borrowed a little here, a little there. Most importantly he evoked the underlying archetypal energies of initiations as a transformative spiritual experience.

You said there was a new level of public activism for Wiccans twenty years ago. What's the difference between that and Gardner going public in the fifties? I thought Wicca became known to mainstream America in the sixties.

Both points were historical breakthroughs that required activists with personal courage. But in the sixties, mainstream America, if they paid any attention, knew Sybil Leek, and my friend Hans Holzer, because they went on television. And they knew Elizabeth Montgomery from *Bewitched*.

What do you think of the stereotype put forward by Bewitched?

Adorable. I love that dress, those heels. Every ten years or so, since the thirties, Hollywood has managed to generate a positive image of the Witch. Dorothy in *The Wizard of Oz* is the epitome of the Witch. She makes the journey and finds she had the power all along. Veronica Lake in *I Married a Witch. Bell, Book, and Candle*, ten years later, Kim Novak. Mischievous, sexy, smart—she went to Vassar. And then Elizabeth Montgomery. She turned the suburban status quo on its ear. That's what Witches do. We are Dionysian. We dance naked around bonfires under the moon. We do think sex is fabulous. We are sexy. So they captured the truth there. Spending the last twenty years trying to banish the negative stereotype in the media, my perspective is that anything that shows the Witch in a positive light is a step forward. The first step is to educate people that Witches don't kill babies, we don't worship Satan. All these images that present Witches as good and attractive help rebut that stereotype. Aside from the green-faced hag, the other big misconception is that Witches have this supernatural power, to cast spells on people. Witches do cast spells, but we don't work with supernatural power. For us, the natural world is full of divine energy. It's natural and it's accessible to us. That's the energy we work with. A spell is like a prayer, except in patriarchal religions, where God is not present in the world, people pray to this father figure to intervene on their behalf. When we cast a spell, we invoke the aid of divinity, and also go into the well of our own innate, divine power, and draw it up, and pour it out into the world. And the most powerful spells are not borrowed from somebody else's book. They are created by you. There are things that have to be learned—practices, techniques, vocabulary, and symbols. It requires devotion and study.

But it's also an innate wisdom, and comes from the heart. So just as you would never pray to harm another person, you would never cast a spell to harm or manipulate another person.

But people do both, I'm sure.

Maybe. I don't run into them practicing Wicca, though. If everything that exists is a manifestation of divine energy, it is logically and spiritually impossible to use that energy to harm. You can use your ego, your misguided self-destructiveness. But those things are the result of not working in harmony with the divine. And it usually backfires. Magic is the way we co-create reality with the sacred. It is not about controlling or manipulating. Shamanism is about ecstasy, the bliss that comes from being connected to the sacred. You can get that by breathing, walking in the country, or making love. Once the veil comes off, your life becomes very magical. In *The Love Spell—*

The book you're writing now?

Right. Love spells can be the trickiest magic there is. Things that we are not aware of influence who we find attractive at a certain point and why. But whether it lasts forever, or you grow apart, it's okay—it's part of the journey to real love. When you make a love spell you're setting the forces in motion so love can manifest. A lot of magic is that capacity to know what the right thing is. We have a preoccupation with manipulation in magical traditions. In most indigenous cultures, ninety percent of what they do is to say, "Thank you. This is good. If you could help us with a little rain, that would be great." It's a posture of asking as opposed to demanding. Prayer is the opening of the heart, an act of optimism that renders a kind of peacefulness, an immediate benefit. That's one reason I love divination. It's a way of engaging in a dialogue with the sacred. Where else can you get that? The mind has phenomenal powers to affect reality—the integrated self working in harmony with the laws of nature, of physics. Quantum laws. We are not defying the laws of nature, but working with them.

In doing so, the religion acknowledges a whole pantheon of Gods and Goddesses. To what level do you interact with them?

To some extent it's a matter of choice, and of their decision to tap you on the shoulder. People ask, "Are the gods psychological forces that dwell within, or do they exist in the outside world?" And my answer is, "Yes."

As a Wiccan, do you tap into Celtic and British tradition?

There are people that do, but I don't focus there. For whatever reason I'm drawn to Italy. If it works, work it. I advocate working with spirits of place, because if the divine is in the world, it is going to express itself very specifically. I don't think it was an accident that the beginning of my Wiccan training corresponded with the beginning of my core shamanic training.

What's "core shamanic"?

The techniques that Michael Harner refined from his work with the Jivarro and other indigenous people. Core practices found in indigenous cultures all over the world, including our ancestors, whether they were Celtic, Greek, African, Native American, or Chinese. These practices alter consciousness, get you out of beta brain waves, which is what we are in right now. The analytical, survival consciousness. There are practices that indigenous cultures and mystical traditions share, to alter the consciousness from beta into alpha, theta, delta—deeper, longer brain waves. In those modes, one is able to apprehend the "magical" nature of reality, and work with those connections. Wherever you find shamanic cultures there is the creation of sacred space, working in a circle, addressing the four directions, invocation, use of prayer, and ecstatic techniques—dancing, fasting, chanting, sleep deprivation, journeying—my favorite is steady percussive rhythm. The priestesses in Egypt used sistrums—rattles. In Greece they used drums. Celtic, Inuit, Japanese, Korean, Siberian, African, and Native American shamans all use drums. It shifts you into an altered state, into non-ordinary reality, where we experience magic and communion with the divine.

In the book you make a pretty definitive statement about not using drugs, but there are traditions that incorporate hallucinogens.

I don't have a moral objection. It's an ancient and appropriate form of shifting consciousness and engaging in Dionysian ecstasy. My problem is the legality. I'm an activist. It was important to me to get these values into the dominant culture, and using drugs might make me vulnerable to arrest. And it's not necessary. There are lots of other techniques to alter consciousness.

How long after you got into that first coven did you start your own?

I trained with my first coven for three years, and about a year later I started my own. There were so few covens that I was pressed into it by people who wanted to study.

Is your original coven around today?

Yes, but with new people. I have relationships with people from way back, but now I'm also working on teaching in new ways with groups all over the world.

You call it the Ara coven. Where does the name come from?

I visited the temple at Paestum in Italy, which is in really marvelous condition compared to other ancient sites. While I was there, I asked for guidance. I was told to "build my temples." I was like, "I live in New York City! Do you have any concept of the cost?" I was stymied, but the seed had been planted.

I was tilling the soil and trying to figure out how to make it grow. Part of magic is perceiving the patterns as they manifest in your life. And if you pay attention, that pattern will tell you your purpose, and how to make magic. That's magic, and most people don't realize it. I tell people, "You want to discover a living universe, you want to make magic? Pay attention to synchronicity, to dreams, and find a method of divination that works. And you are making magic right away. The whole world is going to shift."

So where does the name Ara come from?

I came back from Italy and started paying attention. I came across this ancient shamanic idea that each of us is the place where heaven and earth combine, where the world and the sacred are unified. Each of us is an altar within the temple of our lives. Then I had my astrological chart done, and was told that at the moment I was born, on the horizon was the constellation of Ara within the Zodiacal sign of Scorpio. *Ara* means the *altar*. I was born on the altar. That cinched it. I realized the way to build the temples was by teaching people how to practice so they could become the altars within the temples of their lives.

The way you talk about Italy I assumed you'd taken the name from Aradia.

That was another part of it. I'd been drawn to the story of Aradia. She seems to be a real person who was then mythologized. I expect she was a practitioner of the old religion and a sort of female Robin Hood. She was born around 1313. The 1300s was a period of tremendous volatility in the politics and religion of Europe, and very much so in Italy. The church was beginning to consolidate power. The pressure was on the old religion. Aradia was supposedly raised in Voltaria, outside Florence. She was holding a meeting in Nemi in the Alban hills outside of Rome when there was an attack by the Church's troops. She escaped and disappeared. One story is that in that meeting Aradia's teachings were inscribed on scrolls. They spread these teachings about the divinity of nature and the sacredness of sexuality, and working with the power of the earth. The story goes that the scrolls were seized. There were nine of them, and they were sent to the Pope. But we can't get into the Vatican library, so it's a mystery. Would she have written things down? I doubt it. The shamanic message was always an oral tradition, certainly since the burning of the library in Alexandria.

Charles Leland did a lot of the research into the history of Italian magic, right?

He was an anthropologist before that existed as an academic study. He was American, lived in England, lived in Italy. There's controversy about the material he retrieved. There's a lot of Christian overlay—but that's how it would've evolved. You see that in Santeria, you see it in Voudou. A blending goes on. It makes sense that that would happen. To me, Italy is the lap of the Goddess. There's a powerful move to practice shamanic Wicca over there. I have a hundred people every time I do in these workshops. Whenever I go, I ask them, "Tell me the stories. Tell me what your grandma knew."

Wiccans in current fiction are usually portrayed as following an ancient and unbroken tradition, but you don't claim that. In general, do modern Wiccans believe that?

Oh, some do. But I don't need to be able to point to a continuous initiatory tradition to legitimize what we do. It's the fastest-growing spirituality, not just in the U.S., but in Britain, Canada, and Australia, and the rest of Europe. And it wouldn't be if it didn't bring people into a very intimate and powerful connection to the magic of the divine.

You said the stereotype of the wart-covered hag arose six hundred years ago, during the Inquisition against the Jews. But the crone is a part of every tradition. Different portrayals of Hecate have her as a crone.

Yeah, in contemporary cosmologies. In fact, if you go back far enough, she is depicted as a maiden figure. I was stunned when I explored early Greek mythology. She was not identified with the crone. She has come to be, and I have a theory as to why. The story was that Apollo came to Hecate's priestess, one of the twelve Sibyls, in Cumae on the bay of Naples in Italy, and said, "I will grant you one wish." She scooped up a handful of sand and said, "I want to live as long as there are grains of sand in my hand," but she didn't ask to remain youthful. So she got old. The Sibyl at Cumae was probably a very ancient site. The function of the priestess at Hecate's temple was to take the pilgrim into the underworld and across the River Styx to meet with a deceased relative. She is a very shamanic Goddess—the only one in the Greek pantheon who can move from the underworld to the mortal realm, to the upper, Olympian world. She is actually a surviving Titan, from the previous generation of divinity. In that sense, she is very old. I think over time she came to be depicted as a crone because of that combination of the myth of aging and the actual age of the site going back to Magna Graecia [Great Greece]. The crone is part of the cosmology of the Goddess—the maiden, the mother, and the crone—three phases of womanhood, three phases of the moon. They don't have green faces, and they don't have warts. They don't ride broomsticks in the middle of the night, and they don't eat babies. That stereotype—the way you've got them portrayed on the cover of the book—comes out of the Witch craze. It precisely matches the propaganda against the Jews in the Inquisition. It was an extenstion of those persecutions. The Witch craze began as the Inquisition was ending. The Inquisition had been very successful and the Church didn't want to give up the wealth and power it provided.

What do you think happened in Salem?

Salem was a Pilgrim community, and the persecutions of Witches in Europe were still going on in the 1600s, so it was part of the climate. When you go back and look at the politics and economics, it was much more driven by greed. If you look at the history of the persecutions of the old religion, some of the earliest persecutions were in the 1300s in Italy, and there is no mention of Satan whatsoever, only the mention of the worship of the Goddess Diana.

There were Roman Witch hunts going back to the fourth century.

There were persecutions going back to 3000 B.C. I'm talking about the origins of this stereotype. If you look at the early persecutions, it's only in the late 1400s that the Church links the old religion to Satan. That was not their position initially, because there's no Satan in the old religion, and they knew it. He belongs to the Bible. He's their personification of their own shadow. They need to deal with it instead of projecting it onto other people and then murdering them.

If you go far enough back it's hard to distinguish folklore from fiction. These ideas survived through writers who kept it alive and on the printed page.

In both books I pointed out the continuous subterranean current in western culture, composed of these practices rooted in divine magic. They have different cultural manifestations, but that current is there. You find the romantic poets, the transcendentalists, Goethe, Coleridge, and Wordsworth. Walt Whitman. The progressives of their era. There is always a certain energy, a life force that runs through history and culture.

A life force that wills for change?

The sacred energy. The divine seeking expression in the world, to open our consciousness, so we can realize that we're gods wearing the masks of humans. Scary thoughts to fundamentalists. Scary thoughts to most of us. It's an overwhelming responsibility, but that's the deal. You are a little piece of it. If you don't embrace that, you're cheating yourself of so much fun.

An attorney and Wiccan priestess for almost twenty-five years, H.Ps. Phyllis Curott is author of Witch Crafting: A Spiritual Guide to Making Magic *(Broadway Books, 2001) and the best-selling and internationally acclaimed* Book of Shadows: A Modern Woman's Journey into the Wisdom of Witchcraft and the Magic of the Goddess *(Broadway, 1998), published in thirteen countries. Her new book,* The Love Spell, *is scheduled for release in January 2005 from Gotham Books/Penguin/Putnam. Visit her website at phylliscurott.com for upcoming workshops and to purchase her books.*

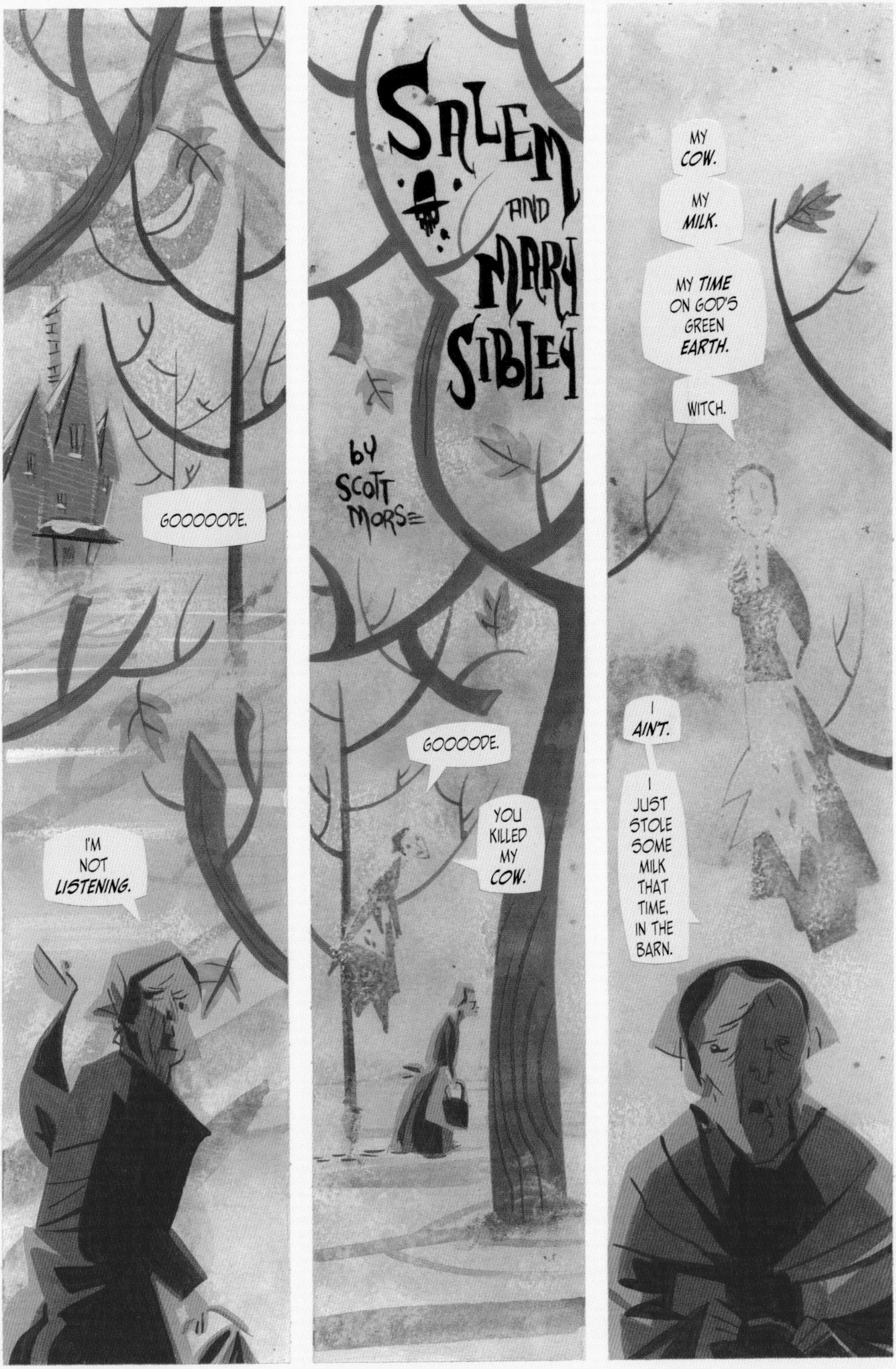
GOOOOODE.
I'M NOT LISTENING.
SALEM AND MARY SIBLEY
by SCOTT MORSE
GOOOODE.
YOU KILLED MY COW.
MY COW.
MY MILK.
MY TIME ON GOD'S GREEN EARTH.
WITCH.
I AIN'T.
I JUST STOLE SOME MILK THAT TIME, IN THE BARN.

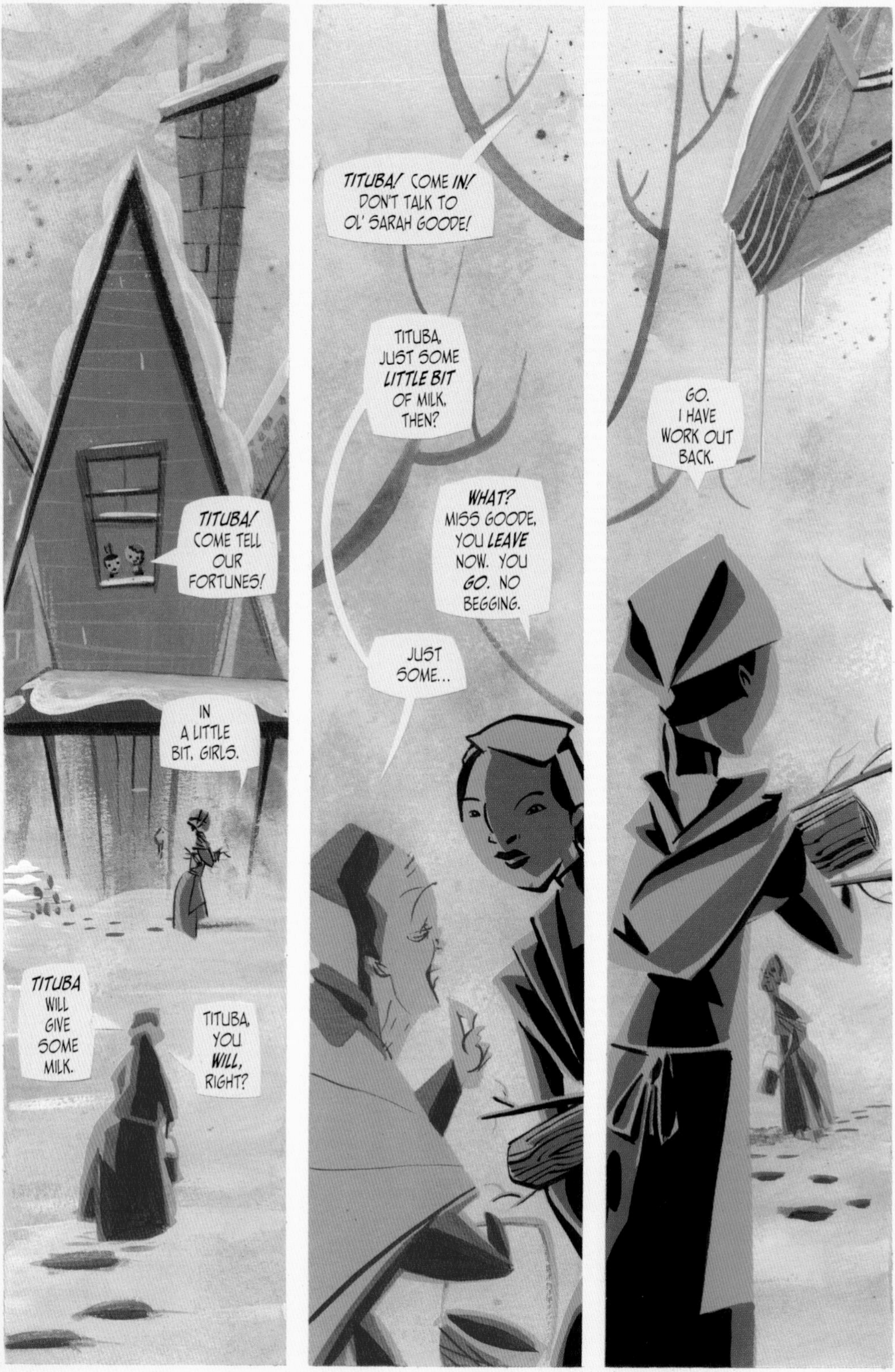
TITUBA! COME TELL OUR FORTUNES!
IN A LITTLE BIT, GIRLS.
TITUBA WILL GIVE SOME MILK.
TITUBA, YOU WILL, RIGHT?
TITUBA! COME IN! DON'T TALK TO OL' SARAH GOODE!
TITUBA, JUST SOME LITTLE BIT OF MILK, THEN?
WHAT? MISS GOODE, YOU LEAVE NOW. YOU GO. NO BEGGING.
JUST SOME...
GO. I HAVE WORK OUT BACK.

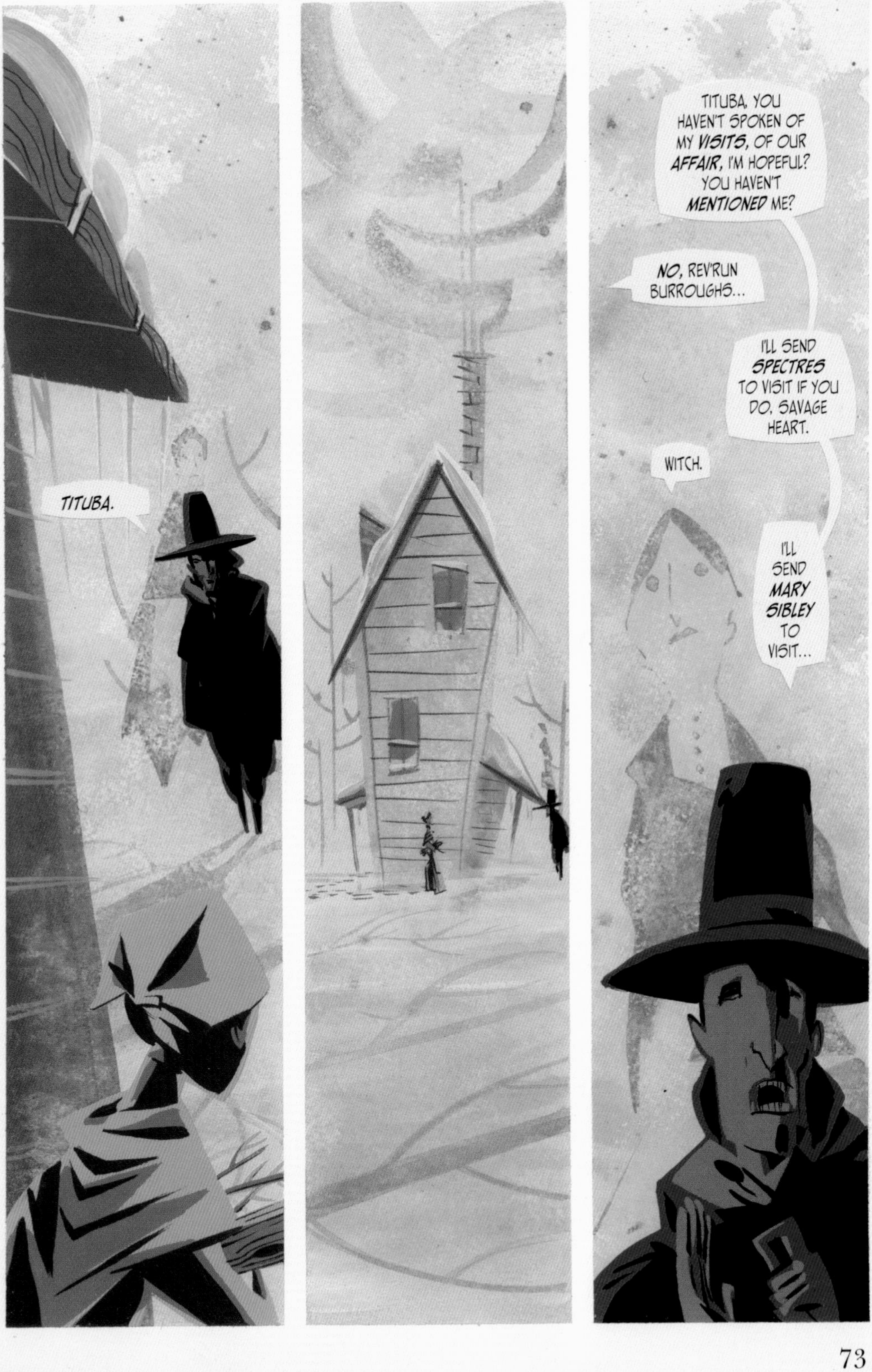
TITUBA.
TITUBA, YOU HAVEN'T SPOKEN OF MY VISITS, OF OUR AFFAIR, I'M HOPEFUL? YOU HAVEN'T MENTIONED ME?
NO, REV'RUN BURROUGHS...
I'LL SEND SPECTRES TO VISIT IF YOU DO, SAVAGE HEART.
WITCH.
I'LL SEND MARY SIBLEY TO VISIT...

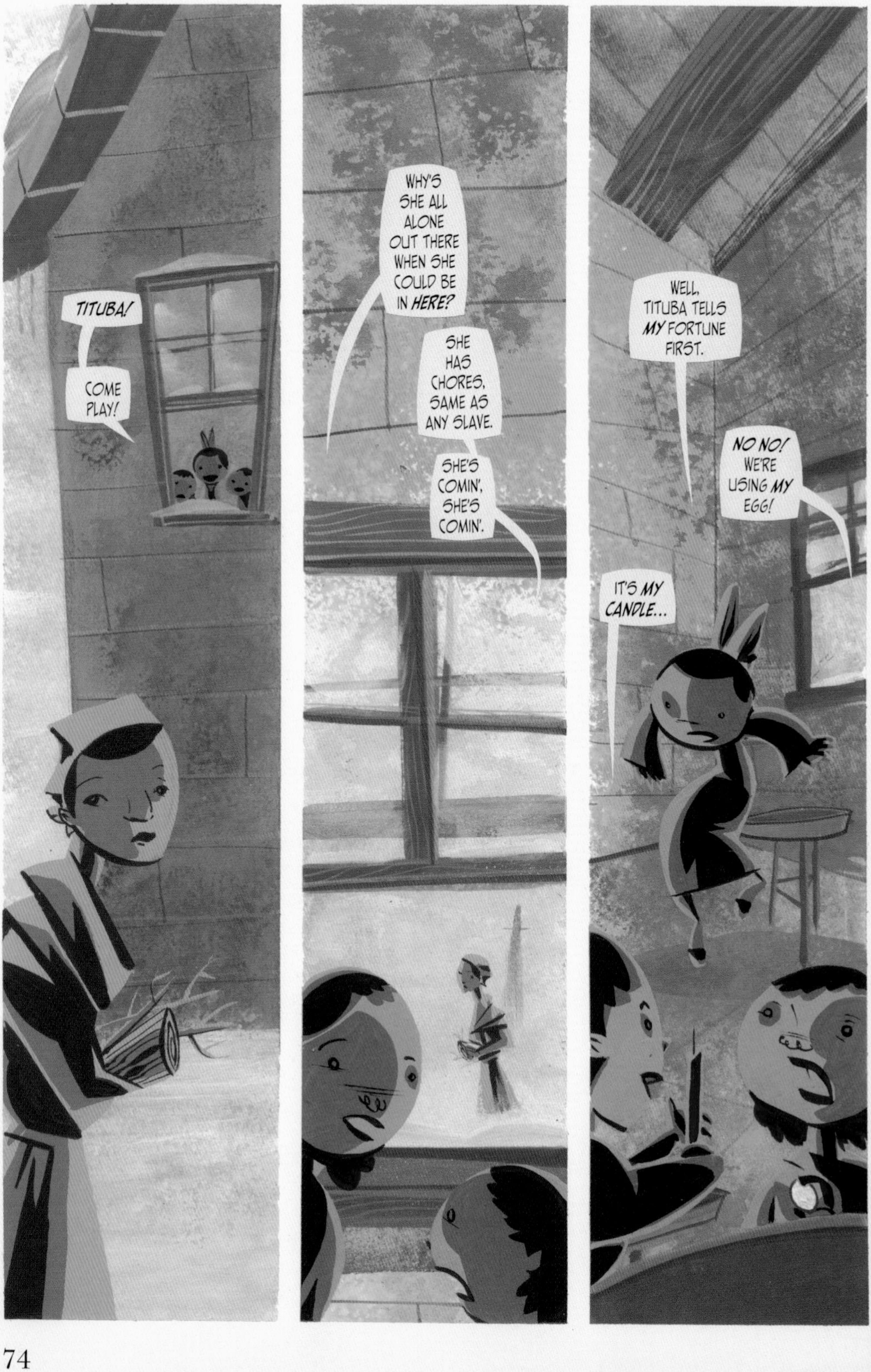
TITUBA!
COME PLAY!
WHY'S SHE ALL ALONE OUT THERE WHEN SHE COULD BE IN HERE?
SHE HAS CHORES, SAME AS ANY SLAVE.
SHE'S COMIN', SHE'S COMIN'.
WELL, TITUBA TELLS MY FORTUNE FIRST.
NO NO! WE'RE USING MY EGG!
IT'S MY CANDLE...

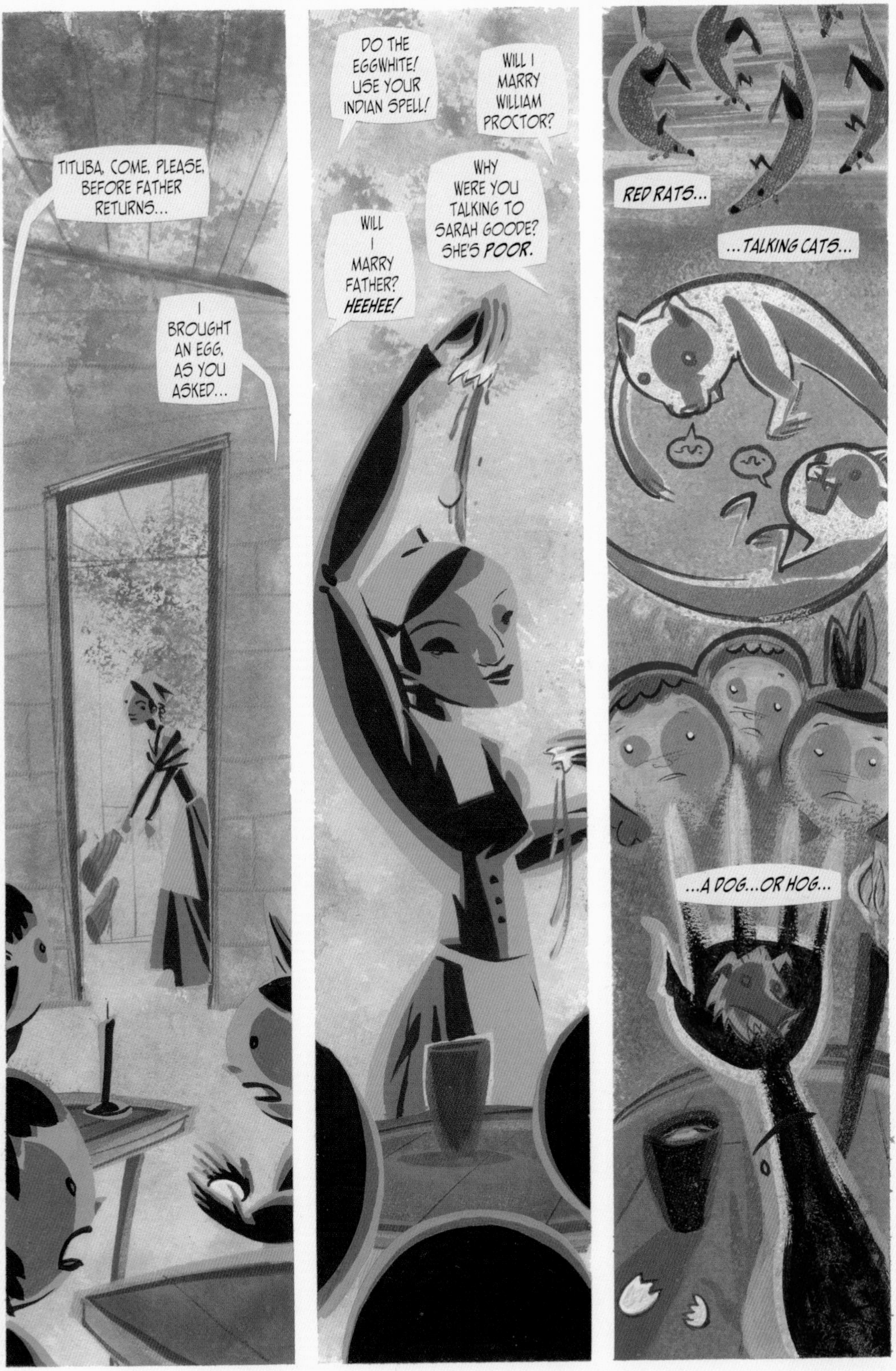
TITUBA, COME, PLEASE, BEFORE FATHER RETURNS...
I BROUGHT AN EGG, AS YOU ASKED...
DO THE EGGWHITE! USE YOUR INDIAN SPELL!
WILL I MARRY WILLIAM PROCTOR?
WHY WERE YOU TALKING TO SARAH GOODE? SHE'S POOR.
WILL I MARRY FATHER? HEEHEE!
RED RATS...
...TALKING CATS...
...A DOG...OR HOG...

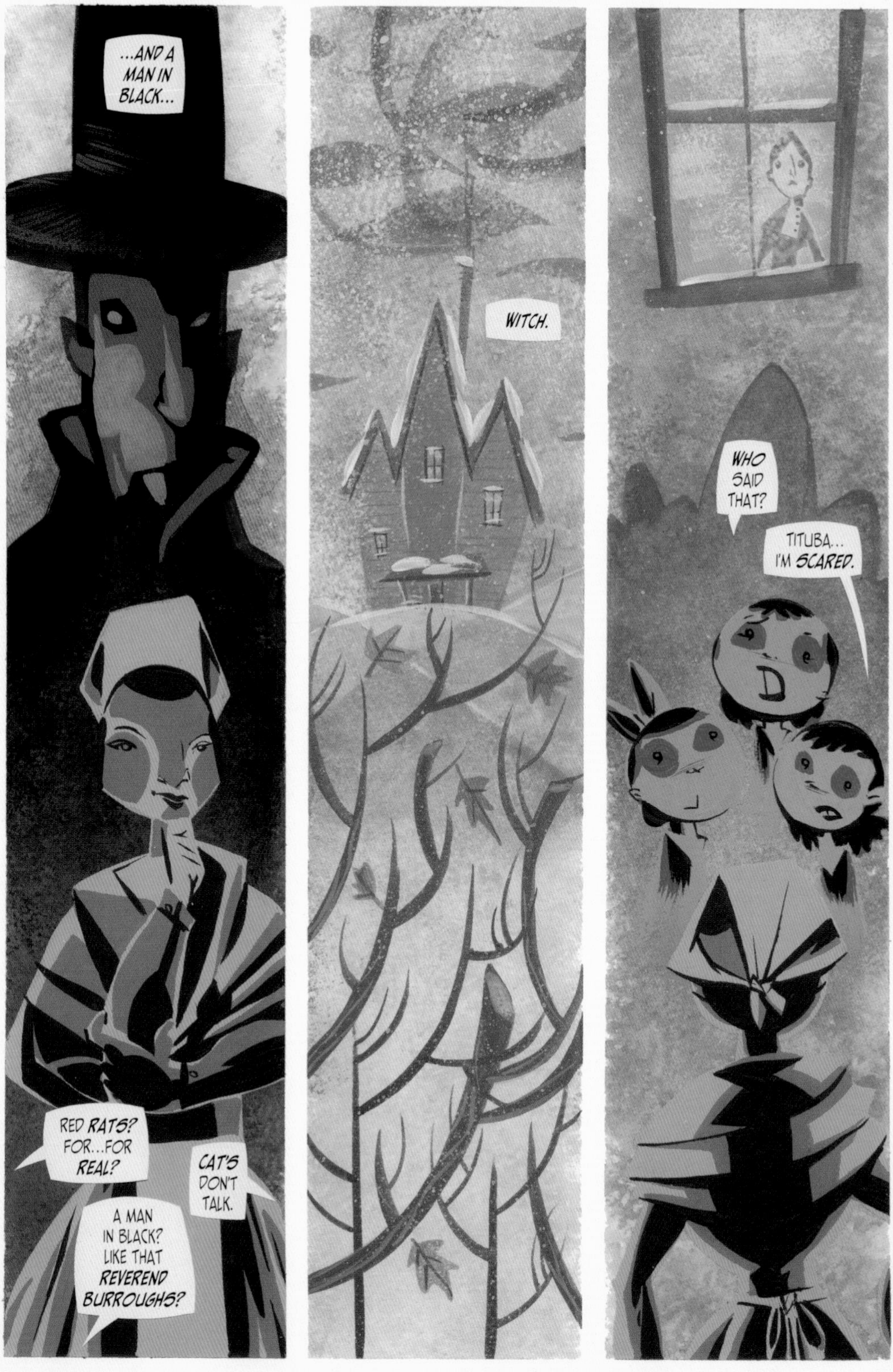
...AND A MAN IN BLACK...
RED RATS? FOR...FOR REAL?
CAT'S DON'T TALK.
A MAN IN BLACK? LIKE THAT REVEREND BURROUGHS?
WITCH.
WHO SAID THAT?
TITUBA... I'M SCARED.

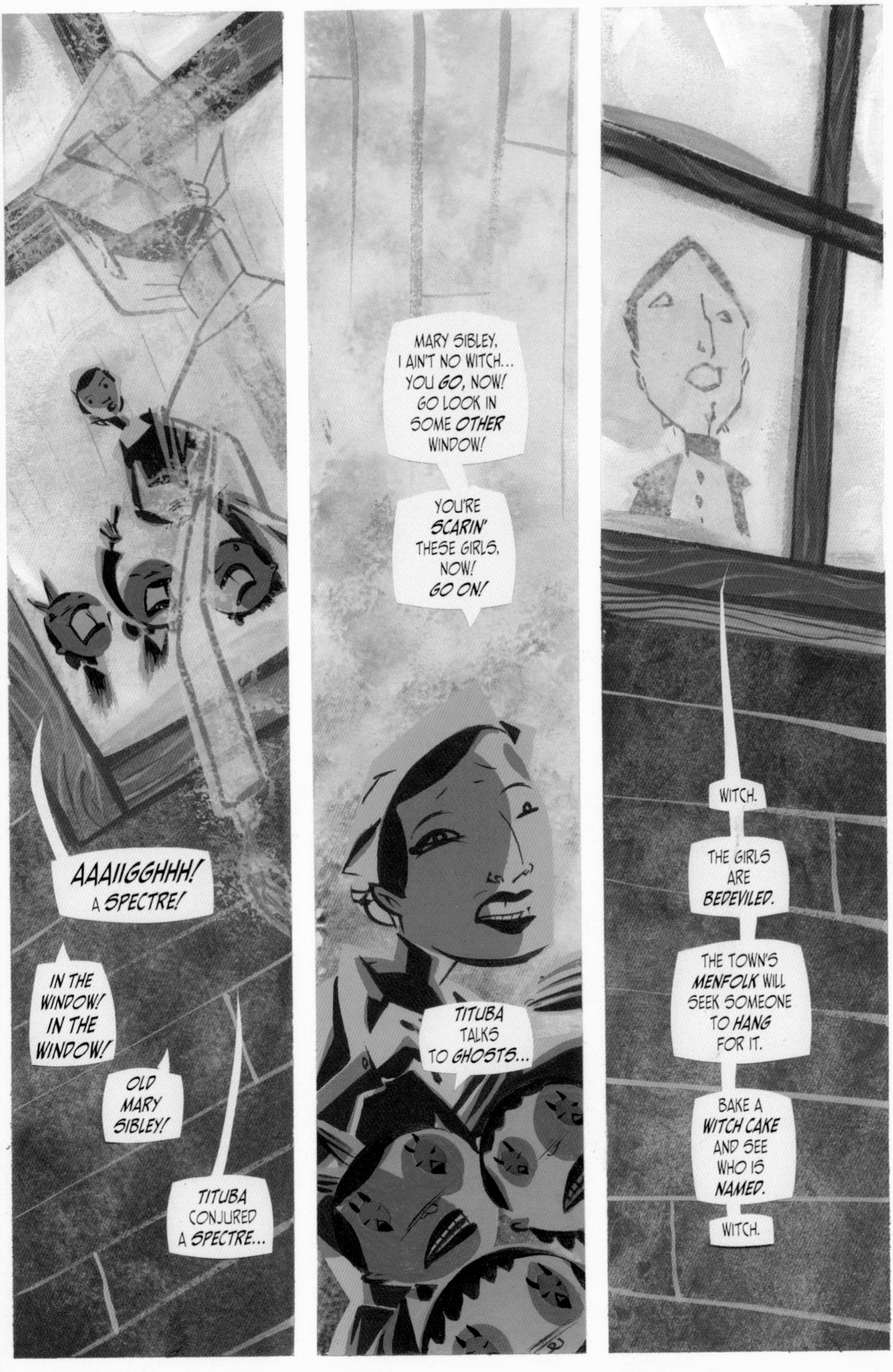
AAAIIGGHHH! A SPECTRE!
IN THE WINDOW! IN THE WINDOW!
OLD MARY SIBLEY!
TITUBA CONJURED A SPECTRE...
MARY SIBLEY, I AIN'T NO WITCH... YOU GO, NOW! GO LOOK IN SOME OTHER WINDOW!
YOU'RE SCARIN' THESE GIRLS, NOW! GO ON!
TITUBA TALKS TO GHOSTS...
WITCH.
THE GIRLS ARE BEDEVILED.
THE TOWN'S MENFOLK WILL SEEK SOMEONE TO HANG FOR IT.
BAKE A WITCH CAKE AND SEE WHO IS NAMED.
WITCH.

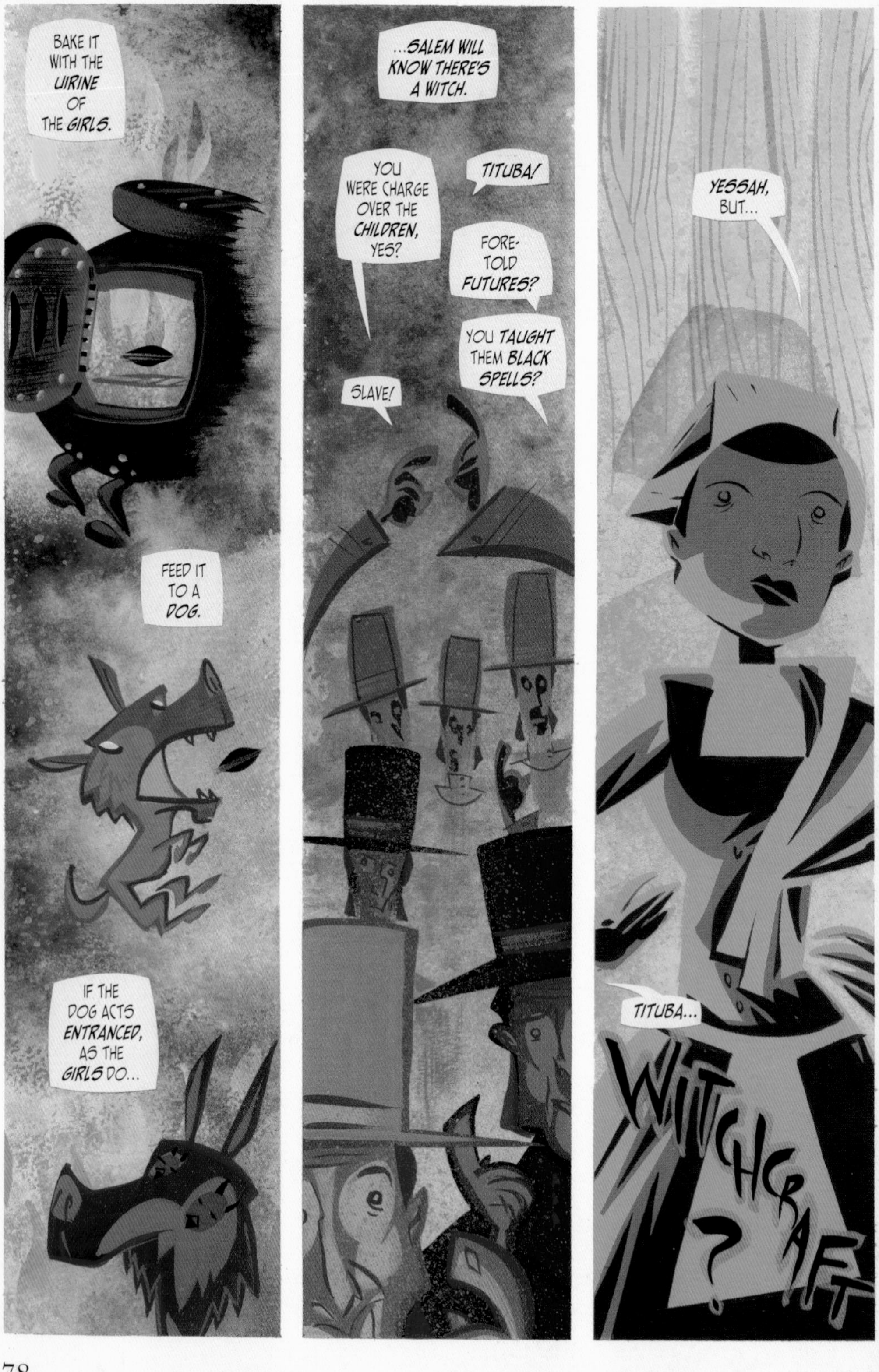
BAKE IT WITH THE URINE OF THE GIRLS.
FEED IT TO A DOG.
IF THE DOG ACTS ENTRANCED, AS THE GIRLS DO...
...SALEM WILL KNOW THERE'S A WITCH.
TITUBA!
YOU WERE CHARGE OVER THE CHILDREN, YES?
FORE-TOLD FUTURES?
YOU TAUGHT THEM BLACK SPELLS?
SLAVE!
YESSAH, BUT...
TITUBA...
WITCHCRAFT?

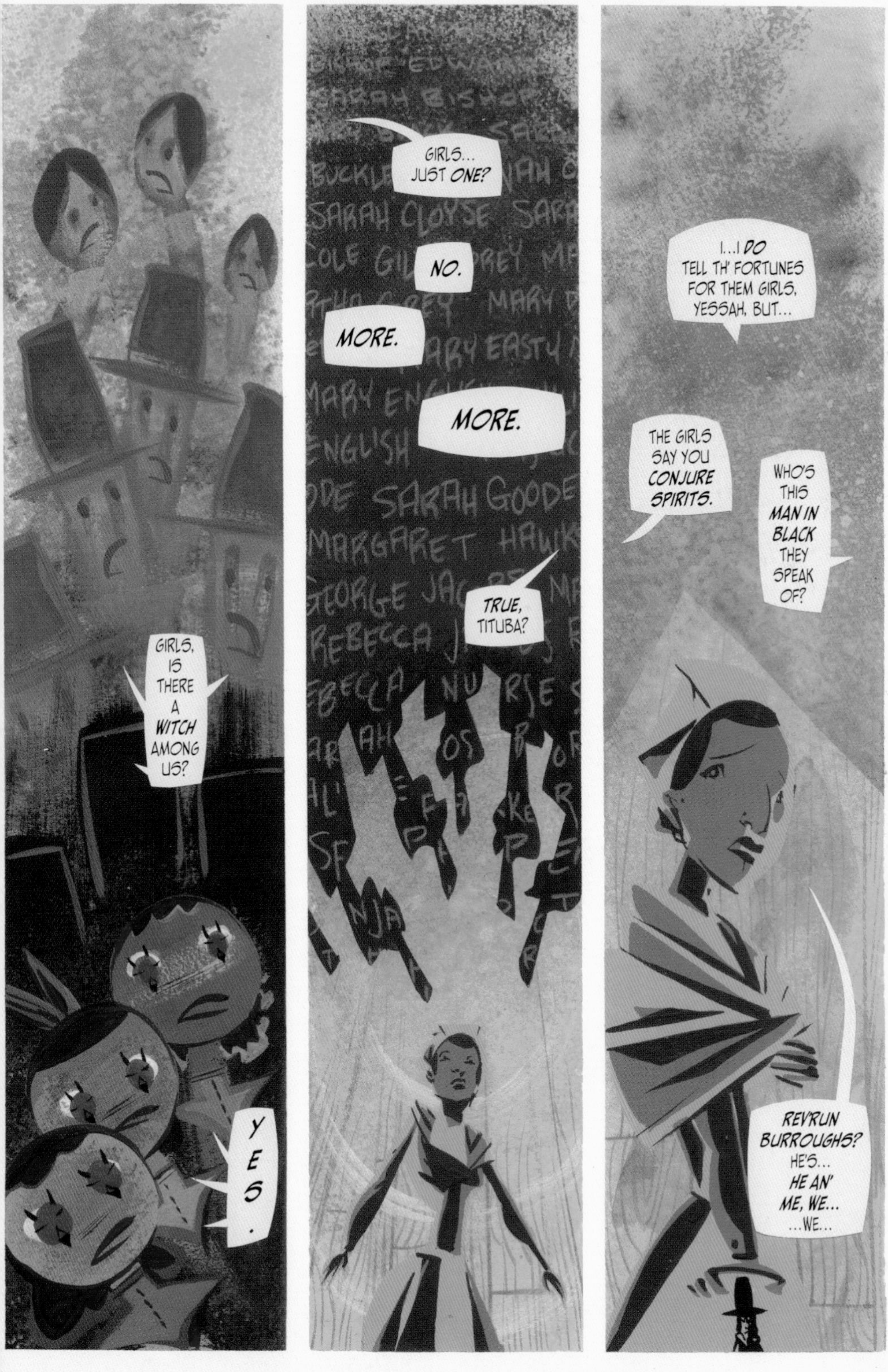
GIRLS, IS THERE A *WITCH* AMONG US?
YES.
GIRLS... JUST *ONE?*
NO.
MORE.
MORE.
TRUE, TITUBA?
I...I *DO* TELL TH' FORTUNES FOR THEM GIRLS, YESSAH, BUT...
THE GIRLS SAY YOU *CONJURE SPIRITS.*
WHO'S THIS *MAN IN BLACK* THEY SPEAK OF?
REV'RUN BURROUGHS? HE'S... *HE AN' ME, WE...* ...WE...

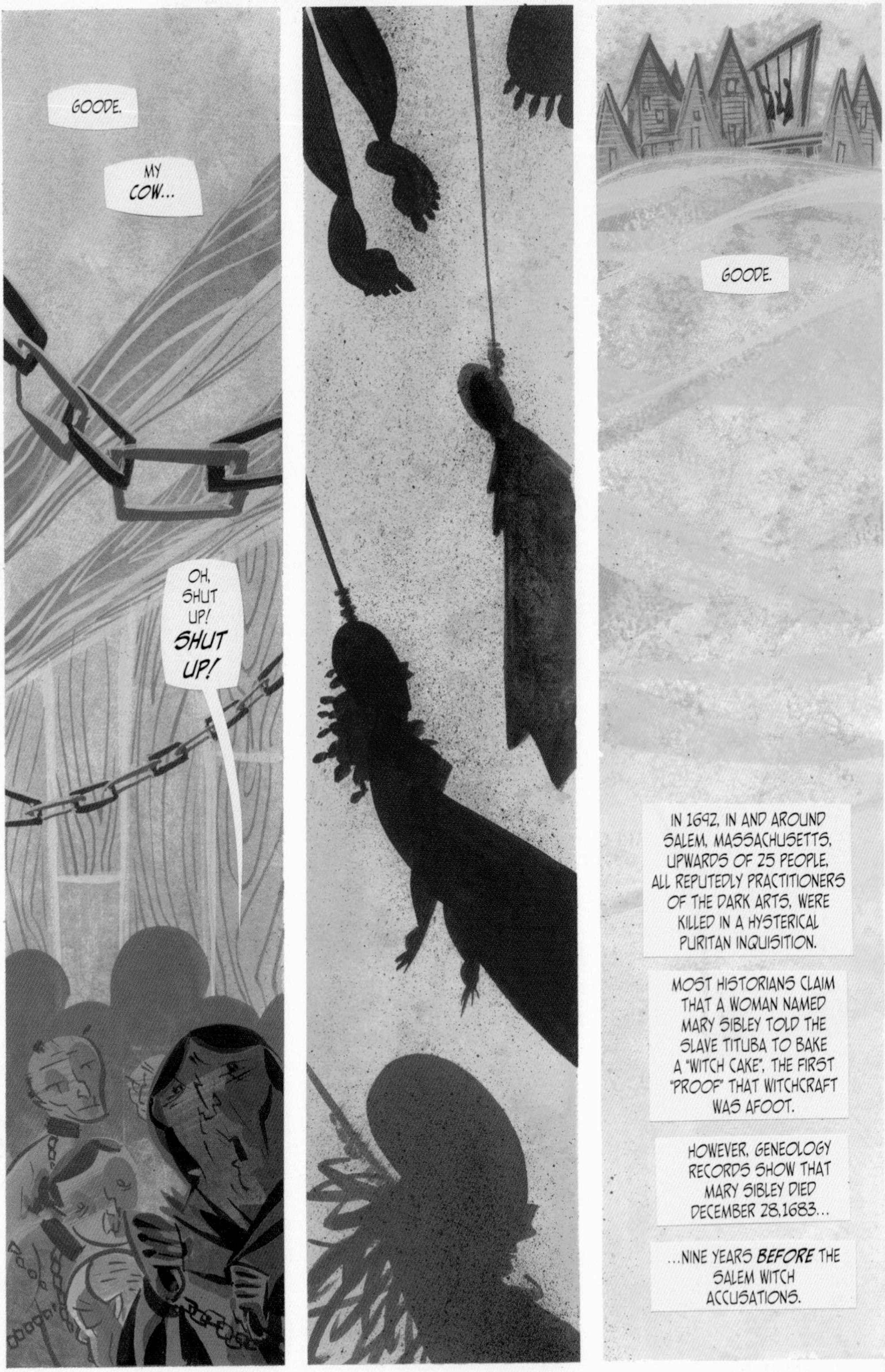
GOODE.
MY COW...
OH, SHUT UP! SHUT UP!
GOODE.
IN 1692, IN AND AROUND SALEM, MASSACHUSETTS, UPWARDS OF 25 PEOPLE, ALL REPUTEDLY PRACTITIONERS OF THE DARK ARTS, WERE KILLED IN A HYSTERICAL PURITAN INQUISITION.
MOST HISTORIANS CLAIM THAT A WOMAN NAMED MARY SIBLEY TOLD THE SLAVE TITUBA TO BAKE A "WITCH CAKE", THE FIRST "PROOF" THAT WITCHCRAFT WAS AFOOT.
HOWEVER, GENEOLOGY RECORDS SHOW THAT MARY SIBLEY DIED DECEMBER 28,1683...
...NINE YEARS BEFORE THE SALEM WITCH ACCUSATIONS.

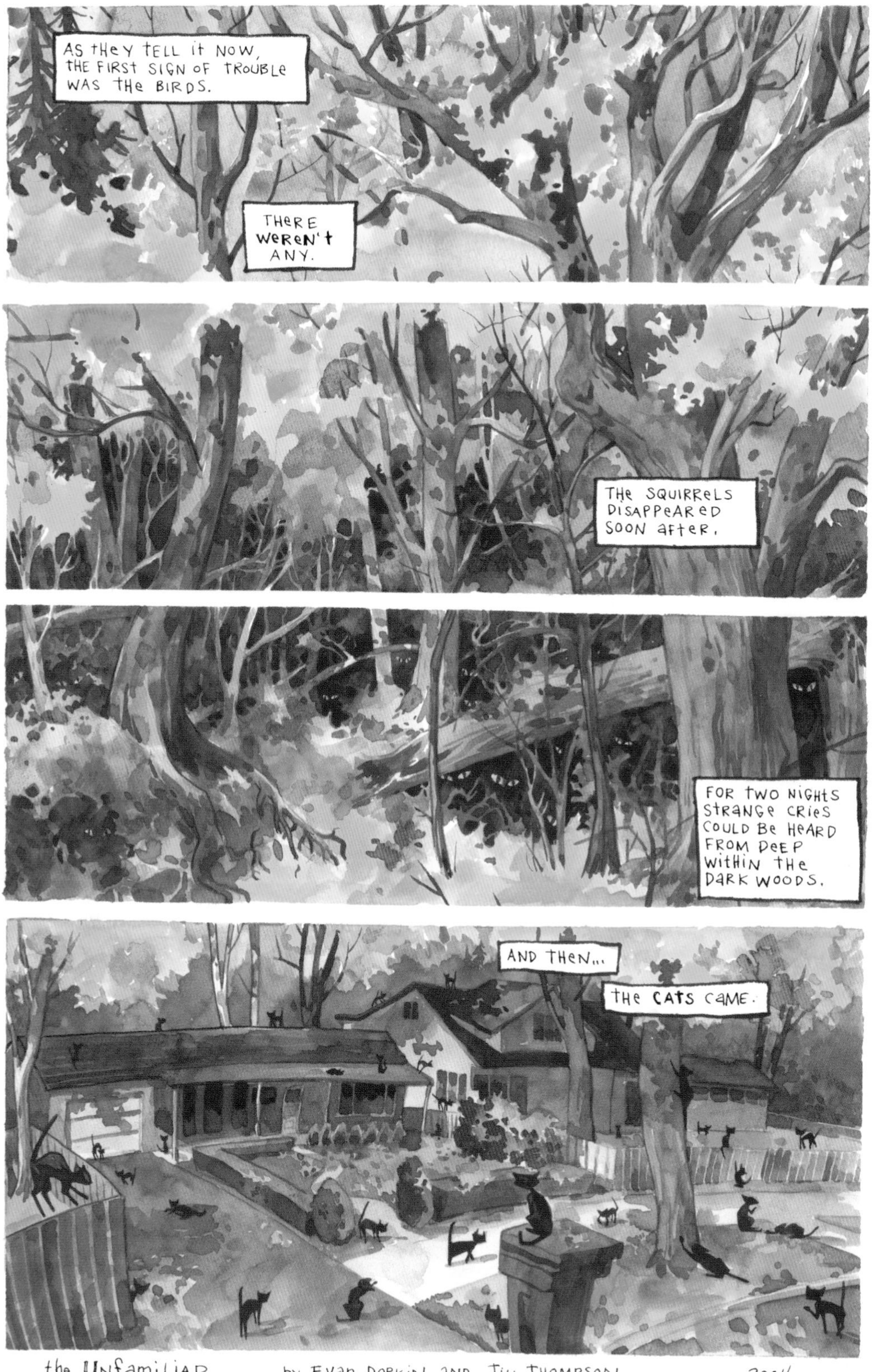
AS THEY TELL IT NOW, THE FIRST SIGN OF TROUBLE WAS THE BIRDS.
THERE WEREN'T ANY.
THE SQUIRRELS DISAPPEARED SOON AFTER.
FOR TWO NIGHTS STRANGE CRIES COULD BE HEARD FROM DEEP WITHIN THE DARK WOODS.
AND THEN...
THE CATS CAME.

the UNFAMILIAR by EVAN DORKIN AND JILL THOMPSON 2004

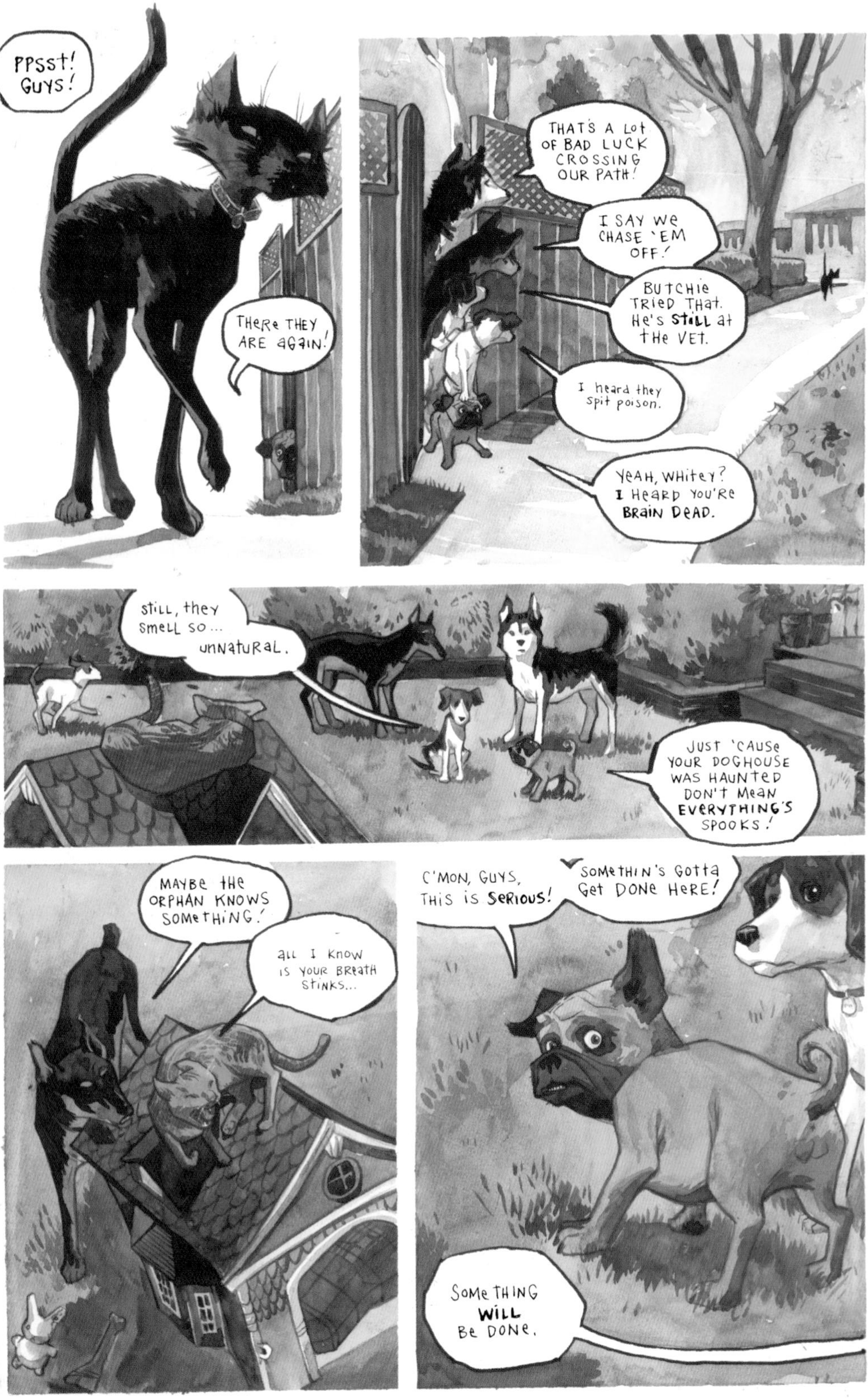
PPSST! GUYS!
THERE THEY ARE AGAIN!
THAT'S A LOT OF BAD LUCK CROSSING OUR PATH!
I SAY WE CHASE 'EM OFF!
BUTCHIE TRIED THAT. HE'S STILL AT THE VET.
I HEARD THEY SPIT POISON.
YEAH, WHITEY? I HEARD YOU'RE BRAIN DEAD.
STILL, THEY SMELL SO... UNNATURAL.
JUST 'CAUSE YOUR DOGHOUSE WAS HAUNTED DON'T MEAN EVERYTHING'S SPOOKS!
MAYBE THE ORPHAN KNOWS SOMETHING!
ALL I KNOW IS YOUR BREATH STINKS...
C'MON, GUYS, THIS IS SERIOUS!
SOMETHIN'S GOTTA GET DONE HERE!
SOMETHING WILL BE DONE.

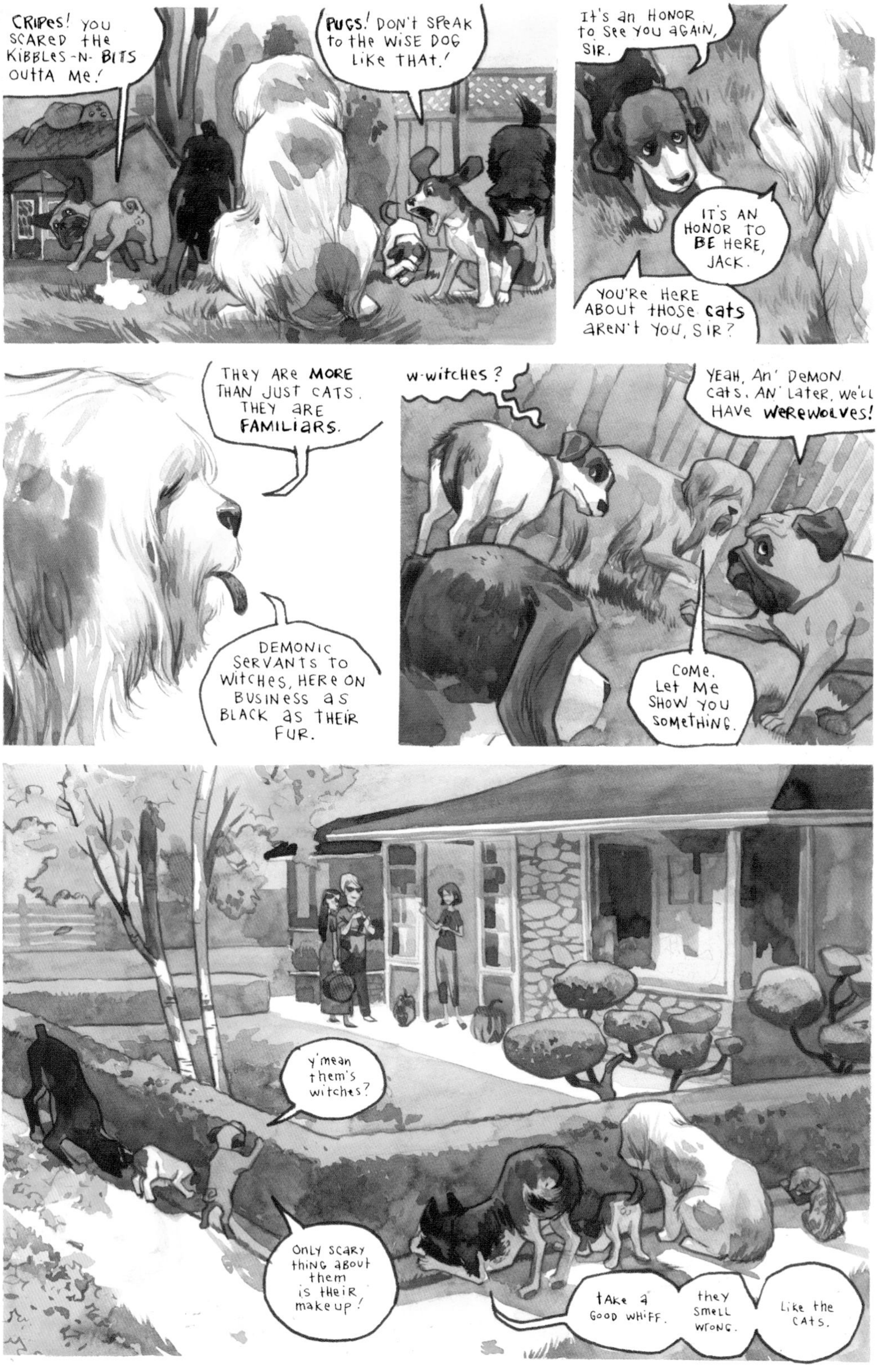
CRIPES! YOU SCARED THE KIBBLES-N-BITS OUTTA ME!
PUGS! DON'T SPEAK TO THE WISE DOG LIKE THAT!
IT'S AN HONOR TO SEE YOU AGAIN, SIR.
YOU'RE HERE ABOUT THOSE CATS AREN'T YOU, SIR?
IT'S AN HONOR TO BE HERE, JACK.
THEY ARE MORE THAN JUST CATS. THEY ARE FAMILIARS.
DEMONIC SERVANTS TO WITCHES, HERE ON BUSINESS AS BLACK AS THEIR FUR.
W-WITCHES?
YEAH, AN' DEMON CATS. AN' LATER, WE'LL HAVE WEREWOLVES!
COME. LET ME SHOW YOU SOMETHING.
Y'MEAN THEM'S WITCHES?
ONLY SCARY THING ABOUT THEM IS THEIR MAKEUP!
TAKE A GOOD WHIFF.
THEY SMELL WRONG.
LIKE THE CATS.

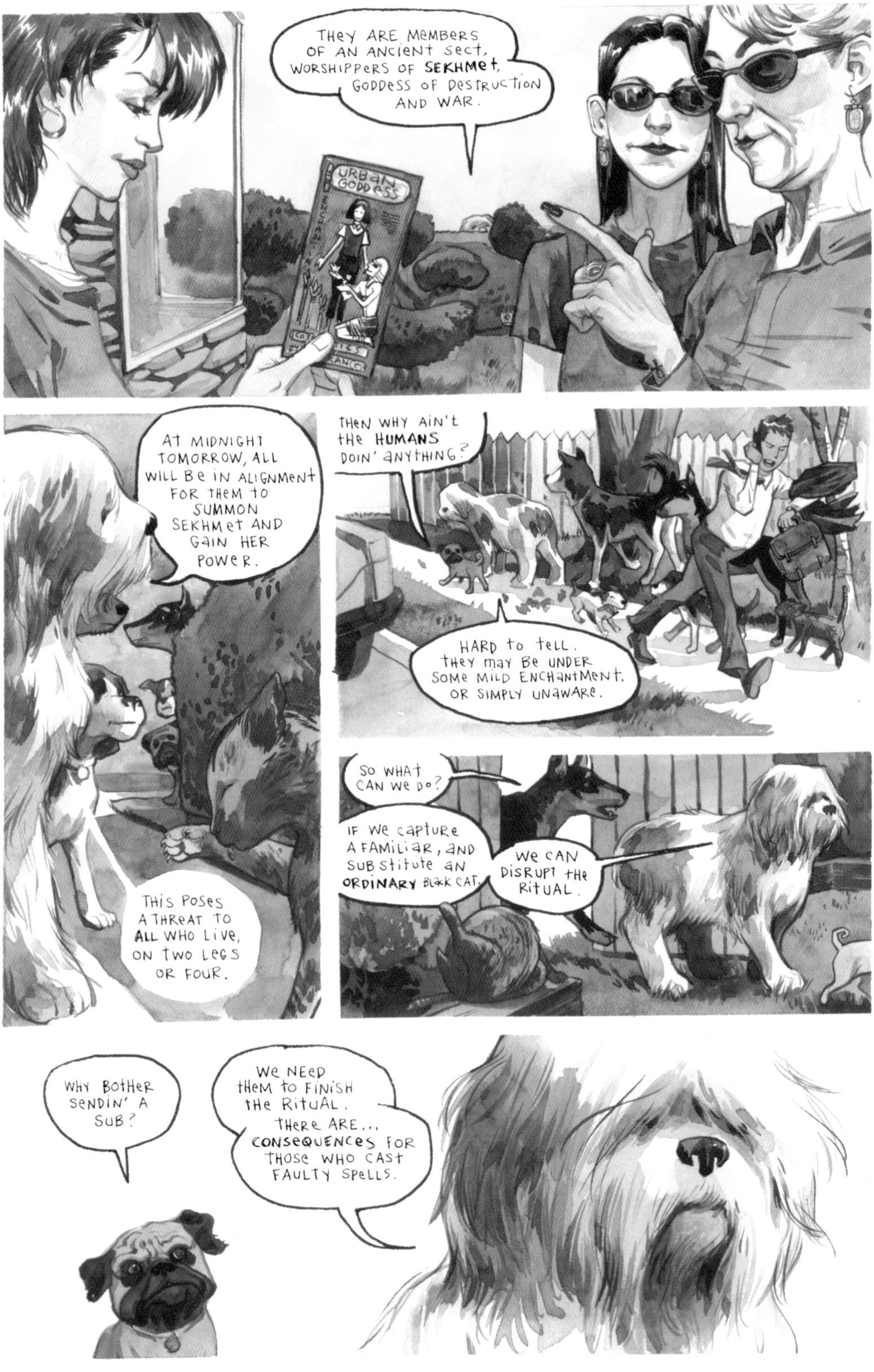
THEY ARE MEMBERS OF AN ANCIENT SECT, WORSHIPPERS OF SEKHMET, GODDESS OF DESTRUCTION AND WAR.
URBAN GODDESS
AT MIDNIGHT TOMORROW, ALL WILL BE IN ALIGNMENT FOR THEM TO SUMMON SEKHMET AND GAIN HER POWER.
THIS POSES A THREAT TO ALL WHO LIVE, ON TWO LEGS OR FOUR.
THEN WHY AIN'T THE HUMANS DOIN' ANYTHING?
HARD TO TELL. THEY MAY BE UNDER SOME MILD ENCHANTMENT, OR SIMPLY UNAWARE.
SO WHAT CAN WE DO?
IF WE CAPTURE A FAMILIAR, AND SUBSTITUTE AN ORDINARY BLACK CAT,
WE CAN DISRUPT THE RITUAL.
WHY BOTHER SENDIN' A SUB?
WE NEED THEM TO FINISH THE RITUAL. THERE ARE... CONSEQUENCES FOR THOSE WHO CAST FAULTY SPELLS.

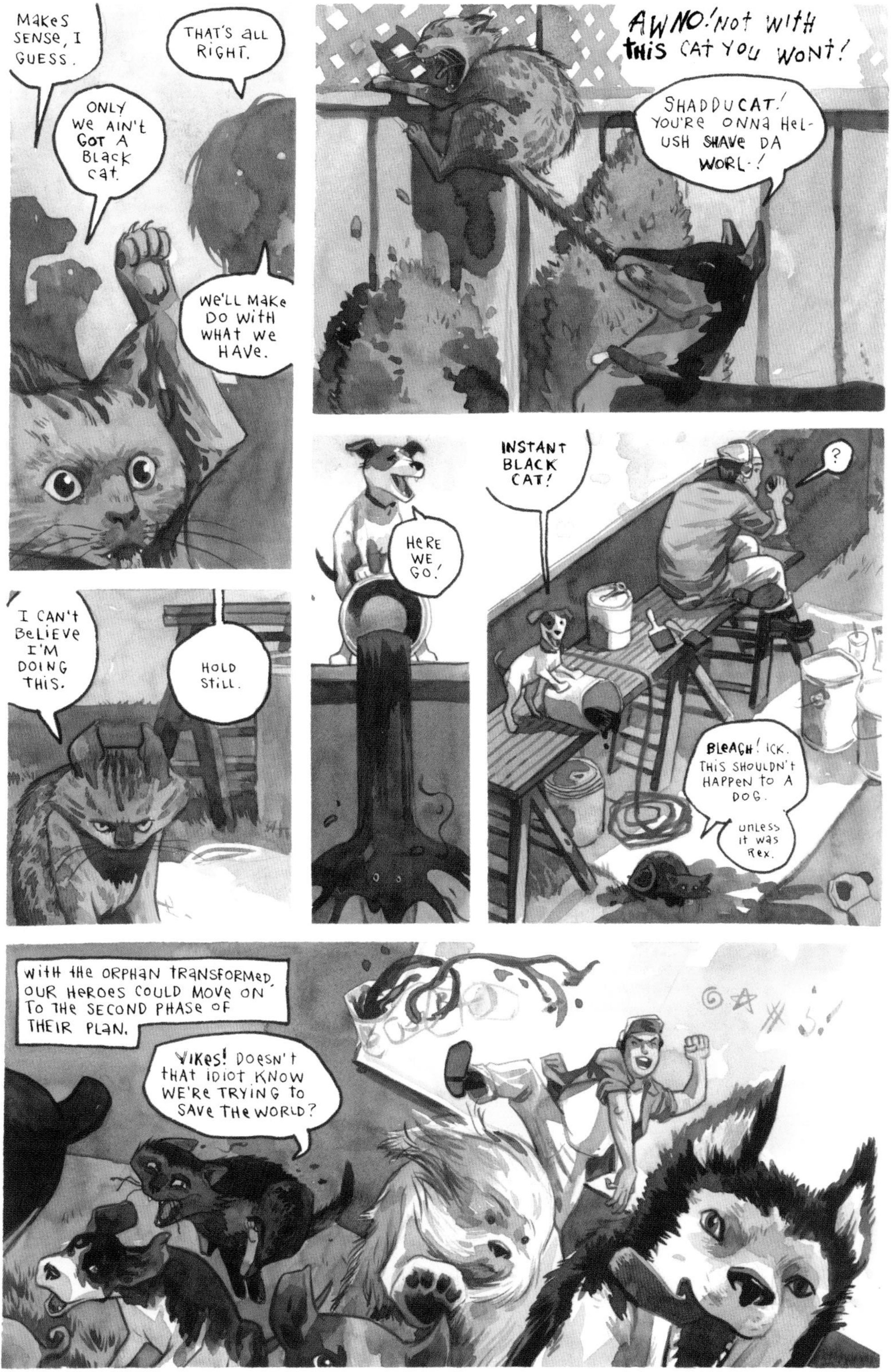

Makes sense, I guess.
That's all right.
Only we ain't got a black cat.
We'll make do with what we have.
AW NO! Not with this cat you won't!
Shadducat! You're onna hel-ush shave da worl-!
Here we go!
Instant black cat!
?
I can't believe I'm doing this.
Hold still.
Bleagh! Ick. This shouldn't happen to a dog.
unless it was Rex.
With the orphan transformed, our heroes could move on to the second phase of their plan.
Yikes! Doesn't that idiot know we're trying to save the world?

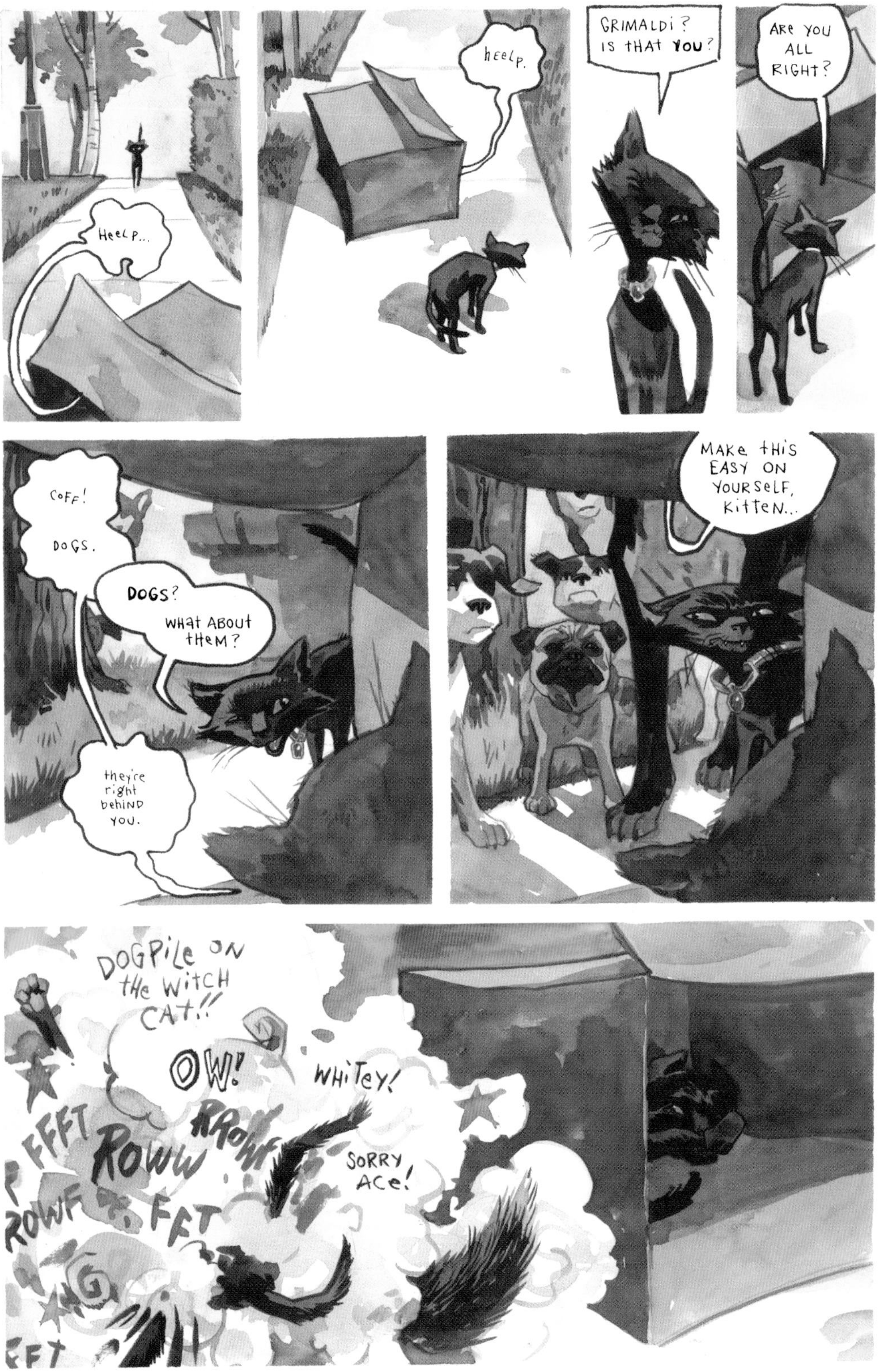
Heelp...
heelp.
GRIMALDI? IS THAT YOU?
ARE YOU ALL RIGHT?
COFF! DOGS.
DOGS? WHAT ABOUT THEM?
they're right behind you.
MAKE THIS EASY ON YOURSELF, KITTEN...
DOGPILE ON THE WITCH CAT!!
OW!
WHITEY!
RROWF
FFFT
ROWW
SORRY ACE!
ROWF
FFT

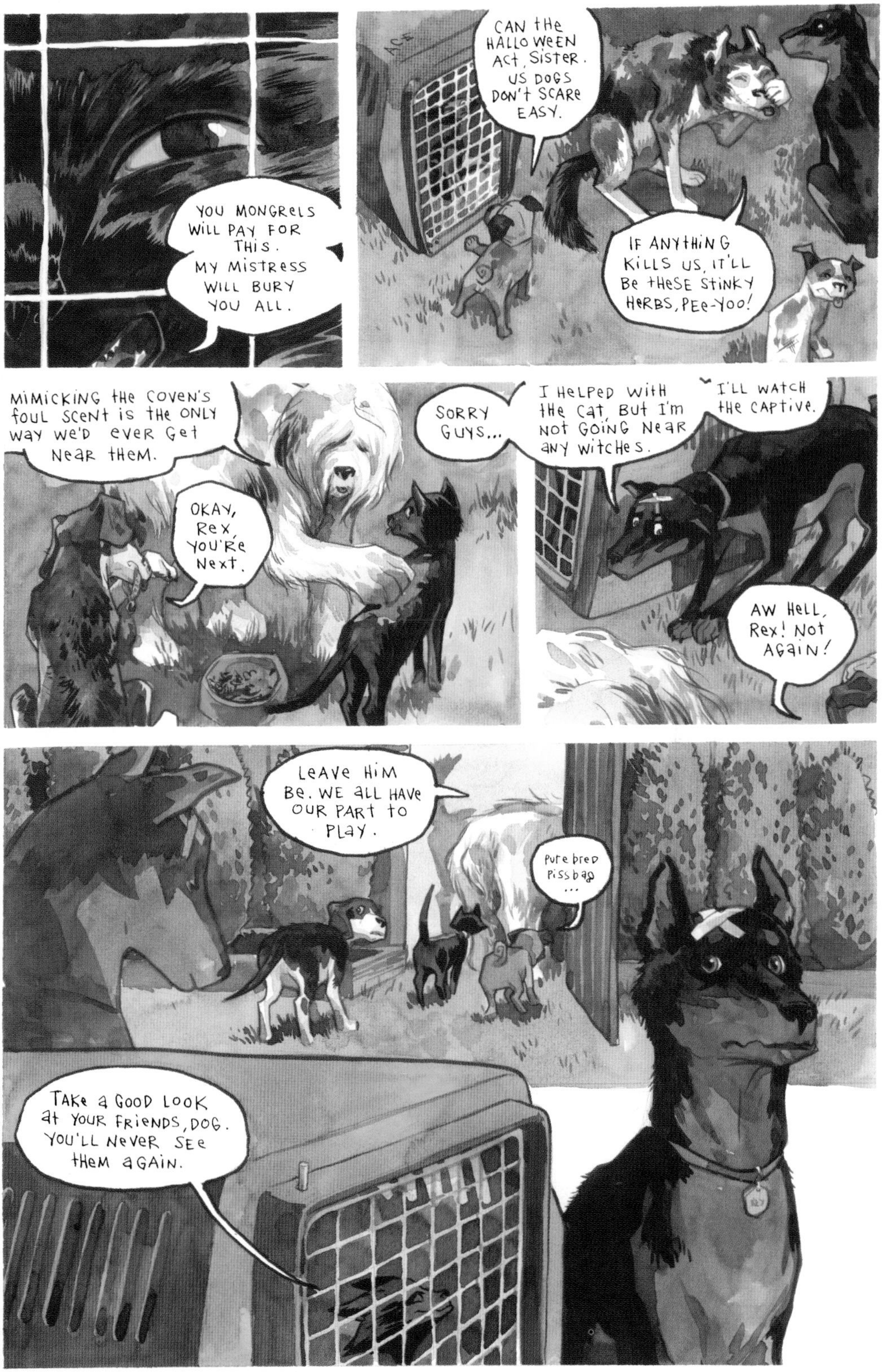
YOU MONGRELS WILL PAY FOR THIS. MY MISTRESS WILL BURY YOU ALL.
CAN THE HALLOWEEN ACT, SISTER. US DOGS DON'T SCARE EASY.
IF ANYTHING KILLS US, IT'LL BE THESE STINKY HERBS, PEE-YOO!
MIMICKING THE COVEN'S FOUL SCENT IS THE ONLY WAY WE'D EVER GET NEAR THEM.
SORRY GUYS...
OKAY, REX, YOU'RE NEXT.
I HELPED WITH THE CAT, BUT I'M NOT GOING NEAR ANY WITCHES.
I'LL WATCH THE CAPTIVE.
AW HELL, REX! NOT AGAIN!
LEAVE HIM BE. WE ALL HAVE OUR PART TO PLAY.
PURE BRED PISSBAG...
TAKE A GOOD LOOK AT YOUR FRIENDS, DOG. YOU'LL NEVER SEE THEM AGAIN.

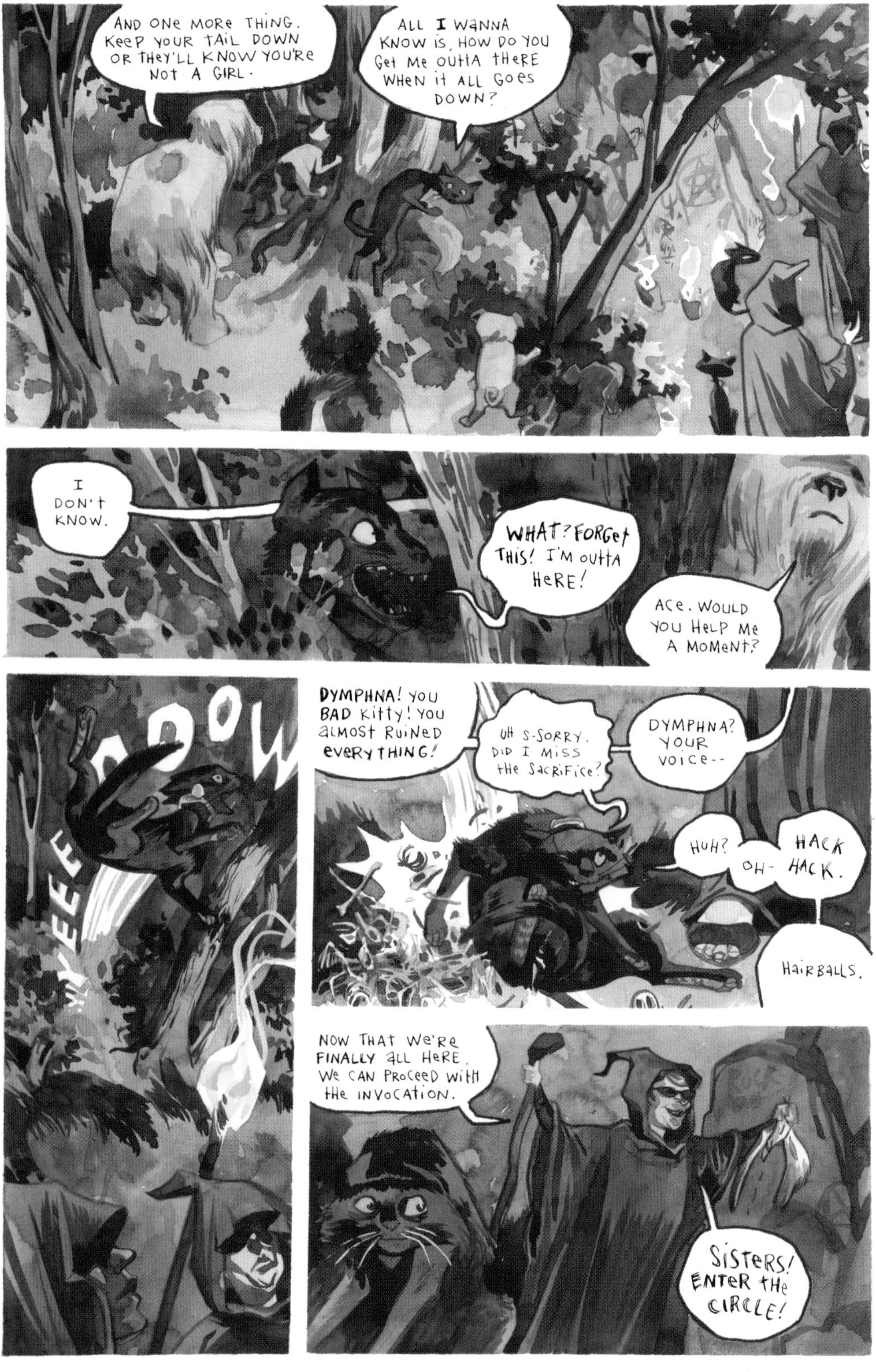
AND ONE MORE THING. KEEP YOUR TAIL DOWN OR THEY'LL KNOW YOU'RE NOT A GIRL.
ALL I WANNA KNOW IS, HOW DO YOU GET ME OUTTA THERE WHEN IT ALL GOES DOWN?
I DON'T KNOW.
WHAT? FORGET THIS! I'M OUTTA HERE!
ACE. WOULD YOU HELP ME A MOMENT?
YEEE OOOW
DYMPHNA! YOU BAD KITTY! YOU ALMOST RUINED EVERYTHING!
UH S-SORRY. DID I MISS THE SACRIFICE?
DYMPHNA? YOUR VOICE--
HUH?
OH-
HACK HACK.
HAIRBALLS.
NOW THAT WE'RE FINALLY ALL HERE, WE CAN PROCEED WITH THE INVOCATION.
SISTERS! ENTER THE CIRCLE!

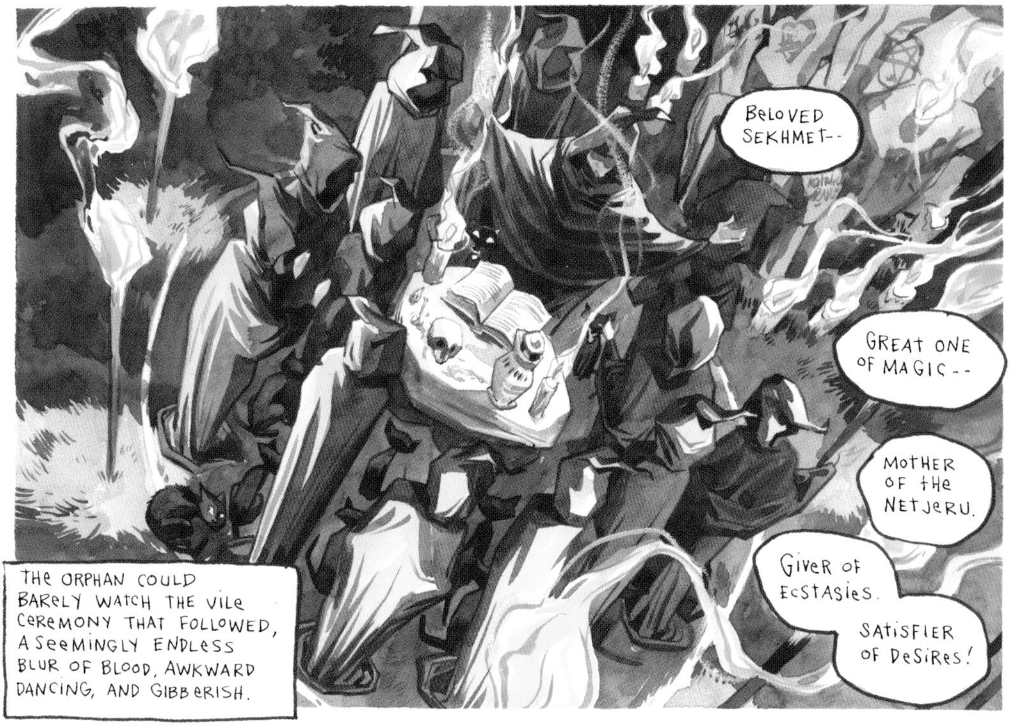
Beloved SEKHMET--
GREAT ONE OF MAGIC--
MOTHER OF THE NETJERU.
Giver of Ecstasies.
SATISFIER OF DESIRES!
THE ORPHAN COULD BARELY WATCH THE VILE CEREMONY THAT FOLLOWED, A SEEMINGLY ENDLESS BLUR OF BLOOD, AWKWARD DANCING, AND GIBBERISH.

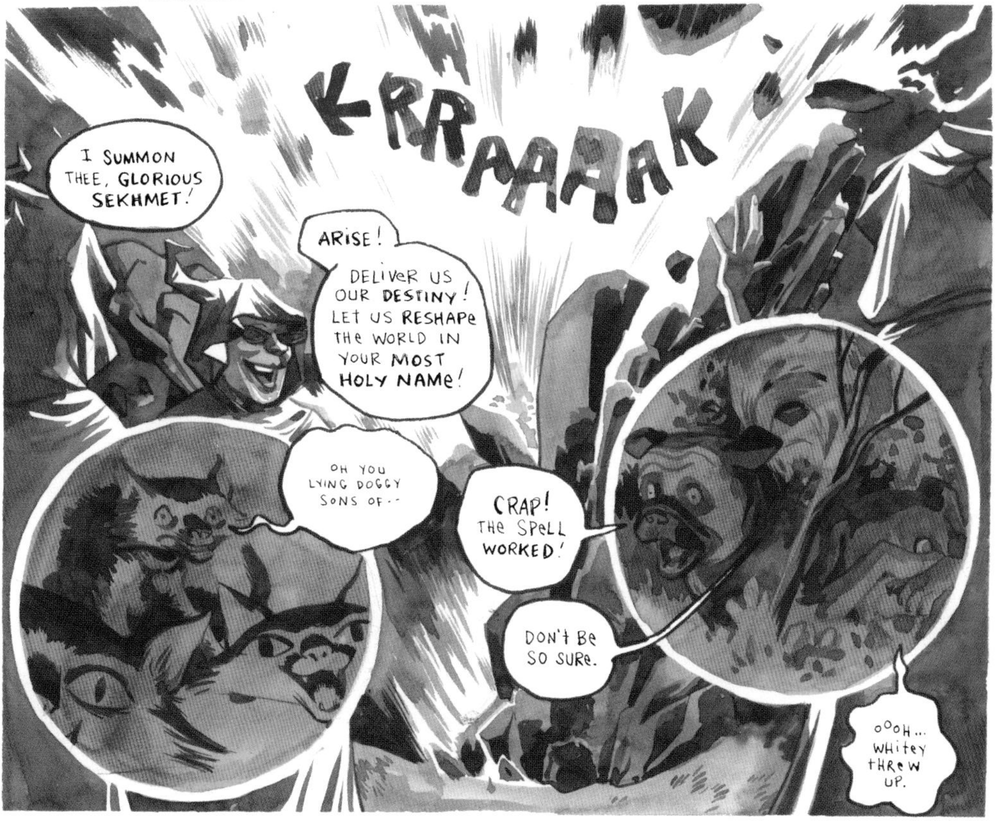
KRRAAAAAK
I SUMMON THEE, GLORIOUS SEKHMET!
ARISE!
DELIVER US OUR DESTINY! LET US RESHAPE THE WORLD IN YOUR MOST HOLY NAME!
OH YOU LYING DOGGY SONS OF--
CRAP! THE SPELL WORKED!
DON'T BE SO SURE.
OOOH... WHITEY THREW UP.

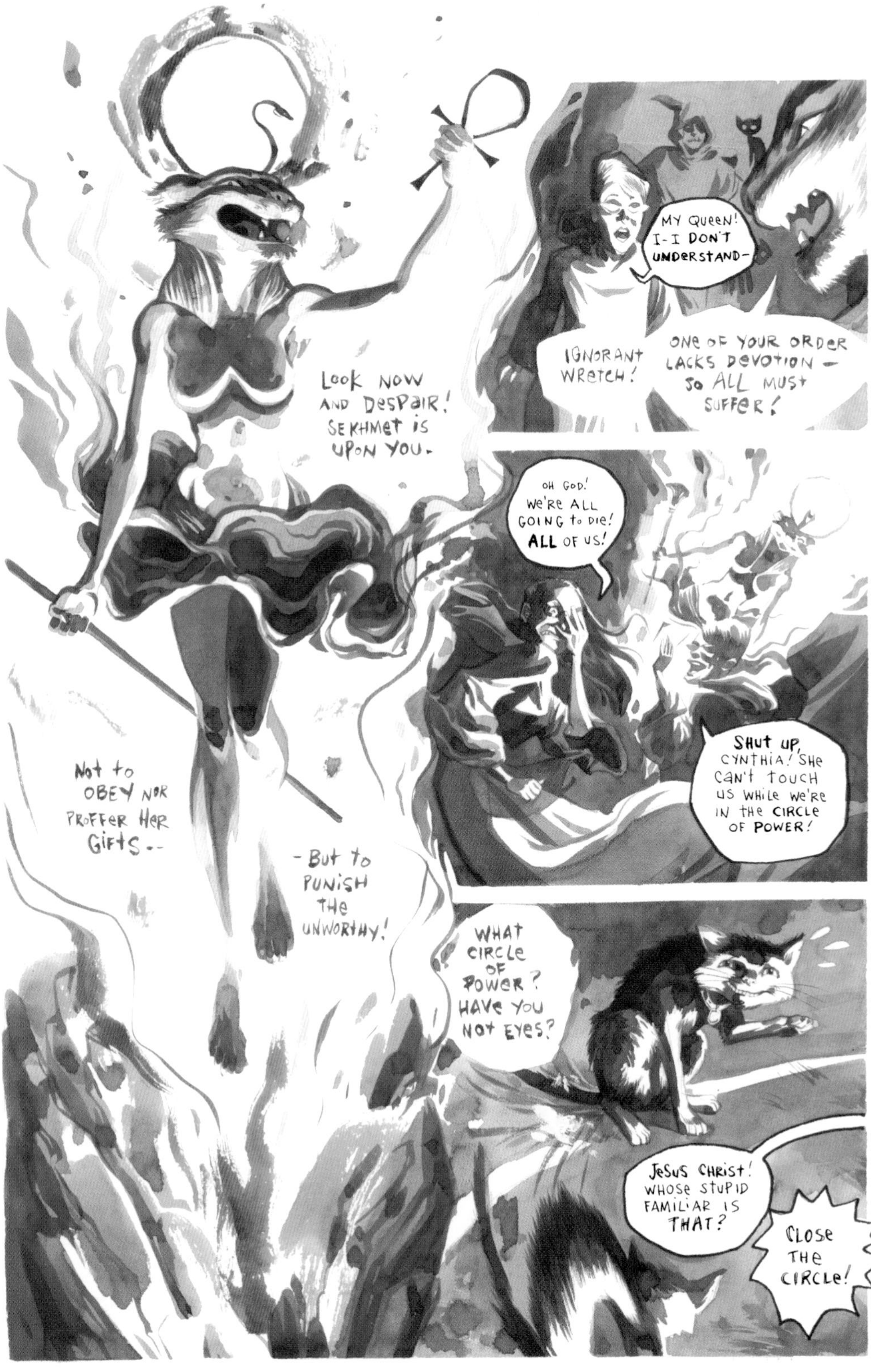
MY QUEEN! I-I DON'T UNDERSTAND-
IGNORANT WRETCH!
ONE OF YOUR ORDER LACKS DEVOTION - SO ALL MUST SUFFER!
LOOK NOW AND DESPAIR! SEKHMET IS UPON YOU.
OH GOD! WE'RE ALL GOING TO DIE! ALL OF US!
SHUT UP, CYNTHIA! SHE CAN'T TOUCH US WHILE WE'RE IN THE CIRCLE OF POWER!
NOT TO OBEY NOR PROFFER HER GIFTS--
-BUT TO PUNISH THE UNWORTHY!
WHAT CIRCLE OF POWER? HAVE YOU NOT EYES?
JESUS CHRIST! WHOSE STUPID FAMILIAR IS THAT?
CLOSE THE CIRCLE!

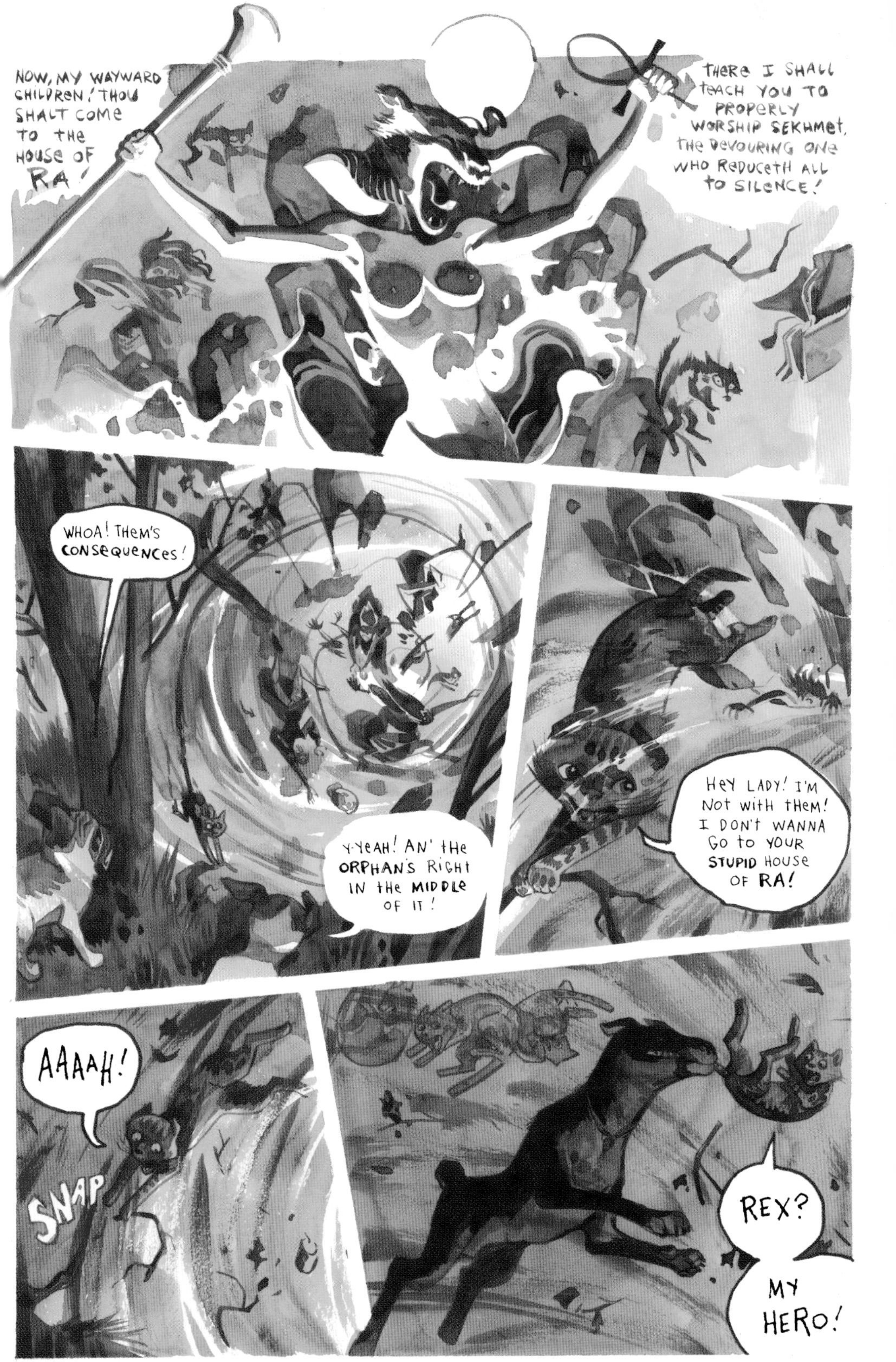
NOW, MY WAYWARD CHILDREN! THOU SHALT COME TO THE HOUSE OF RA!
THERE I SHALL TEACH YOU TO PROPERLY WORSHIP SEKHMET, THE DEVOURING ONE WHO REDUCETH ALL TO SILENCE!
WHOA! THEM'S CONSEQUENCES!
Y-YEAH! AN' THE ORPHAN'S RIGHT IN THE MIDDLE OF IT!
HEY LADY! I'M NOT WITH THEM! I DON'T WANNA GO TO YOUR STUPID HOUSE OF RA!
AAAAH!
SNAP
REX?
MY HERO!

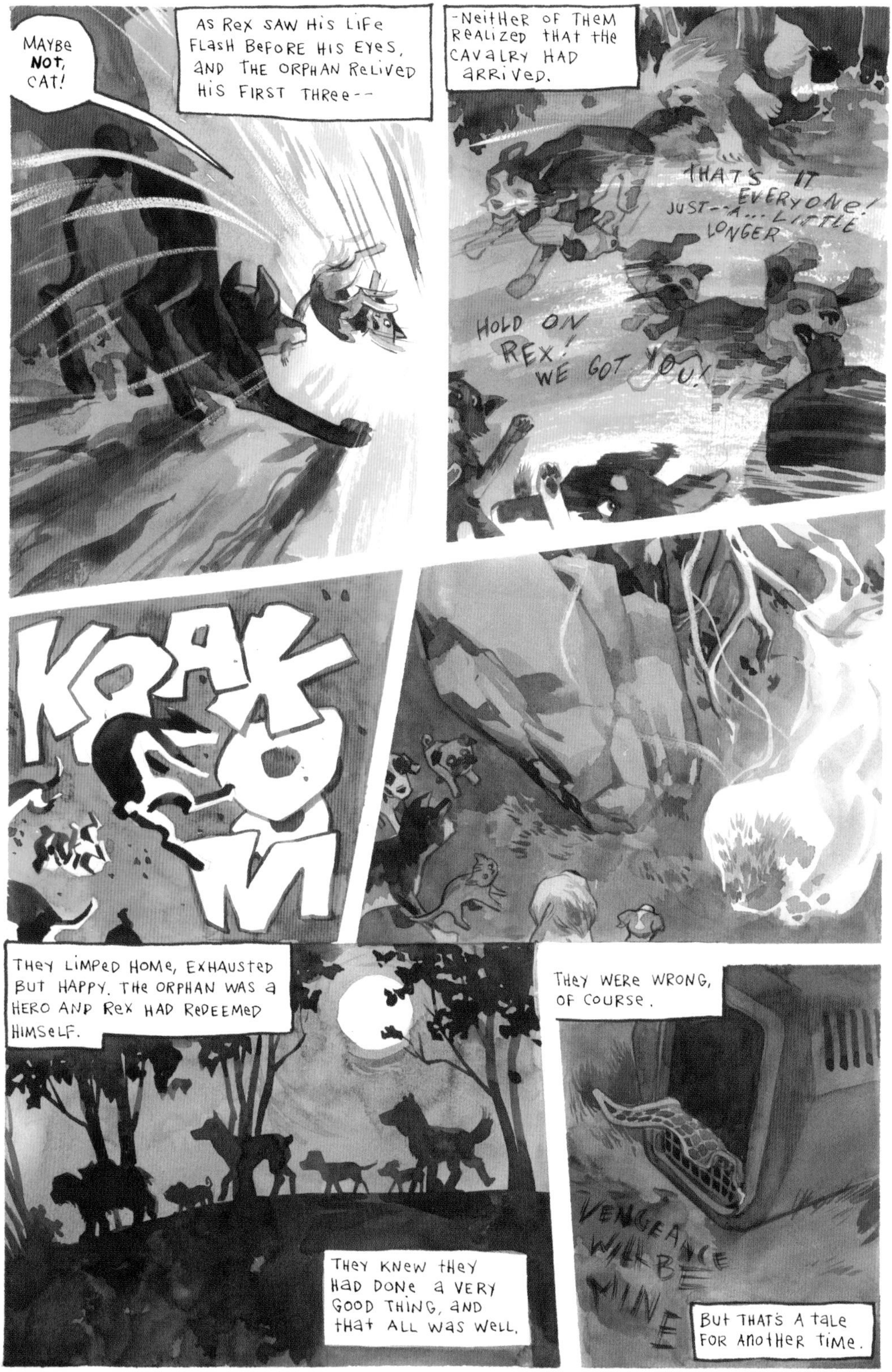
MAYBE NOT, CAT!
AS REX SAW HIS LIFE FLASH BEFORE HIS EYES, AND THE ORPHAN RELIVED HIS FIRST THREE--
-NEITHER OF THEM REALIZED THAT THE CAVALRY HAD ARRIVED.
THAT'S IT EVERYONE! JUST--A...LITTLE LONGER
HOLD ON REX! WE GOT YOU!
KRAKOOM
THEY LIMPED HOME, EXHAUSTED BUT HAPPY. THE ORPHAN WAS A HERO AND REX HAD REDEEMED HIMSELF.
THEY KNEW THEY HAD DONE A VERY GOOD THING, AND THAT ALL WAS WELL.
THEY WERE WRONG, OF COURSE.
VENGEANCE WILL BE MINE
BUT THAT'S A TALE FOR ANOTHER TIME.

Our Artists and Writers

TONY MILLIONAIRE grew up in the seaside town of Gloucester, Massachusetts, where his grandparents taught him to draw ships and old houses. After spending thousands of Sunday afternoons gazing at his grandfather's collection of old newspaper comics, he picked up a pen and started drawing monkeys with striped tails and top hats. He now writes and draws the weekly strip *Maakies* (www.maakies.com) as well as the comic book *Sock Monkey*, which has won him four Eisner Awards including Best Writer/Artist, Humor in 2003. He lives in Pasadena, California with his wife and daughters.

WILLIAM SHAKESPEARE is the celebrated author of *Romeo and Juliet*, *MacBeth*, *Hamlet*, and many other plays, poems, and sonnets. This is his first work for Dark Horse.

MIKE MIGNOLA is among the most highly regarded writer/artists of horror comics today, which is a unique distinction for someone whose work can be as humorous as it is frightening. He has also worked in film and television, with Francis Ford Coppola on *Bram Stoker's Dracula*, and as a production designer on *Disney's Atlantis: The Lost Empire*. He was also Visual Consultant to Guillermo del Toro on *Blade 2* and the *Hellboy* feature film. Mignola lives in New York City.

GARY GIANNI graduated from The Chicago Academy of Fine Arts in 1976. His artwork has appeared in the *Chicago Tribune*, numerous magazines, children's books, and paperbacks. Gianni debuted his work in the comics field in 1990 and has since been recognized with the Eisner Award for Best Short Story. He is perhaps best known for his ink drawing and oil paintings for a number of book collections including *The Savage Tales of Solomon Kane*, which is now available at book stores in a trade paperback edition published by Del Ray. Gianni also draws Hal Foster's classic comic strip *Prince Valiant* appearing every Sunday in over 300 newspapers nationally.

Descended from Norman-French nobles and Lancashire crusaders, **CLARK ASHTON SMITH** (1893 – 1961) completed only five years of formal education. At seventeen, he began selling stories to *The Black Cat* and other magazines. Like his contemporaries Robert E. Howard and H. P. Lovecraft, it was his publication in *Weird Tales* which led to real success. In his sixty-eight years Smith worked as a journalist, a sculptor, a painter, a fruit picker and packer, a wood chopper, a typist, a cement mixer, a gardener, a miner, a mucker, and a windlasser. The version of "Mother of Toads" in this volume has been published only once before—in a small chapbook issued from Necronomicon Press in 1987. The text is from Smith's working manuscripts, and is different from the text that appeared in the July 1937 issue of *Weird Tales*, and all subsequent publications.

PAUL LEE is a painter and freelance illustrator, the creator of the comics series *Lurid*, and co-creator of *The Devil's Footprints*. He has worked closely with Brian Horton, most notably on Dark Horse's *Buffy the Vampire Slayer* covers. He recommends fiber to promote regularity, and lives with his wife and son in Southern California.

BRIAN HORTON has been an illustrator and video-game artist for ten years. He's worked for interactive companies including Disney, Dreamworks, and Electronic Arts (EA). At EA he was the Lead Artist on *Clive Barker's Undying*, and for the past two years has been at The Collective, art directing *Indiana Jones and the Emperor's Tomb*. Brian moonlights in comics with his partners in crime, Scott Allie and Paul Lee, on *Buffy*, *Star Wars*, and *The Devil's Footprints*. He shares his life with his wife Susan and son Victor in Aliso Viejo, California.

SCOTT ALLIE writes and edits comics and stories for Dark Horse Comics and other publishers. He lives in Portland, Oregon with his wife Melinda and their phantom cat, Shadow.

JIM and RUTH KEEGAN have been compensating for each other artistically since the mid-eighties when they co-art directed *Comics Feature* magazine. They've since collaborated as storyboard artists, editorial cartoonists, and advertising illustrators. Jim received a 2003 Eisner nomination for his publication design of Gary Gianni's *Corpus Monstrum*. Currently, Jim and Ruth are producing "The Adventures of Two-Gun Bob," a series of biographical vignettes based on the life of pulp author Robert E. Howard, for Dark Horse's new *Conan* comic. They live in Los Angeles with their son Rourke.

SEAN PHILLIPS has been drawing comics for over twenty years for every major publisher. After ten years drawing people standing around talking for various Vertigo comics including *Hellblazer*, *The Invisibles*, *The Minx*, and *Hell Eternal*, he branched out into drawing superheroes standing around talking, including *Batman*, *Wildcats*, *Uncanny X-Men*, and *Sleeper*.

MARK RICKETTS is dead. However, he continues to annoy the living by producing graphic novels like *Nowheresville* and *Whiskey Dickel, Int'l Cowgirl* from the grave. He is also working on the graphic novel, *Lazarus Jack* with artist Horacio Domingues. Can no one stop this monster?

SCOTT MORSE is the author of multiple graphic novels and short stories, including *Soulwind* (Oni Press), *The Barefoot Serpent* (Top Shelf Productions), *Southpaw* (AdHouse Books), and *Ancient Joe* (Dark Horse). In animation, he's acted as designer, storyboard artist, writer, art director, and producer for Univeral, Cartoon Network, Disney, and Nickelodeon. He lives in Burbank, California, but would rather be backpacking in Yosemite. He knows how to get to Hanging Basket, but it's a secret worth keeping, so don't ask for directions.

JILL THOMPSON is a renowned illustrator and the creator of the award-winning, all-ages cartoon-book series *Scary Godmother*. Her work has been seen in books ranging from *Classics Illustrated* and *Wonder Woman* to *Sandman*. Jill is a longtime resident of Chicago, where she lives with her husband, the comic-book writer Brian Azzarello.

EVAN DORKIN is the Harvey, Eisner, and Ignatz Award-winning creator of *Milk and Cheese* and *Dork* from Slave Labor Graphics, and various Marvel, Dark Horse, and DC comics. His cartooning has appeared in *Esquire*, *Spin*, *The Onion*, *Disney Adventures*, and *Nickelodeon* magazine. With Sarah Dyer, he's written for *Space Ghost Coast to Coast*, *Superman*, and *Batman Beyond*, and was creator, writer, and executive producer of *Welcome to Eltingville*, his very own failed pilot that aired on Cartoon Network's Adult Swim block. He is currently working on his next failed pilot for them.

ALSO FROM DARK HORSE COMICS!

Mike Mignola
P. Craig Russell
Jill Thompson
Evan Dorkin
Paul Chadwick
Gary Gianni
and others
The Dark Horse Book of
HAUNTINGS

THE DARK HORSE BOOK OF HAUNTINGS HC
Featuring Mike Mignola, P. Craig Russell, Paul Chadwick, Evan Dorkin, Jill Thompson, and others. Cover by Gary Gianni

Mike Mignola's Hellboy investigates a haunted house and discovers his own unexpected connection to the spirits within. P. Craig Russell and Mike Richardson tell the story of a child who vanishes into an abandoned house, and Paul Chadwick and Randy Stradley team up for a creepy short about a haunted suit. Jill Thompson and Evan Dorkin recount the legend of a haunted doghouse.

Hard cover, 96 pages, Full color
$14.95, ISBN: 1-56971-958-6

HELLBOY
THE BOOK THAT INSPIRED THE MOTION PICTURE!
SEED of DESTRUCTION
MIKE MIGNOLA ◆ JOHN BYRNE

HELLBOY VOLUME 1: SEED OF DESTRUCTION
By Mike Mignola and John Byrne

When strangeness threatens to engulf the world, a strange man will come to save it. Sent to investigate a mystery with supernatural overtones, Hellboy discovers the secrets of his own origins, and his link to the Nazi occultists who promised Hitler a final solution in the form of a demonic avatar.

Soft cover, 128 pages, Full color
$17.95, ISBN: 1-59307-094-2

THE COLLECTED WORKS of TONY MILLIONAIRE'S
Sock Monkey
VOLUMES THREE and FOUR

COLLECTED WORKS OF TONY MILLIONAIRE'S SOCK MONKEY VOLUMES 3-4
By Tony Millionaire

Here is a beautiful collection of work from Eisner Award winner Tony Millionaire. This book collects his latest four comic books, including the scandalous issue in which Uncle Gabby is so distraught over the accidental killing of a baby bird that he attempts suicide.

Soft cover, 88 pages, b&w
$12.95, ISBN: 1-59307-098-5

C. SCOTT MORSE
ANCIENT JOE
•el bizarron•

ANCIENT JOE
By C. Scott Morse

He never should've taken the Devil's silver. Now his wife's passed away, and though Joe fears the worst—that she's a captive of El Diablo—Joe follows a path that leads him through the afterlife and beyond to find her. A God? Myth? Man? Who can know? Not a soul, but Ancient Joe ...

Soft Cover, 120 pages, b&w
$12.95, ISBN: 1-56971-795-8

AVAILABLE AT YOUR LOCAL COMICS SHOP OR BOOKSTORE • To find a comics shop in your area, call 1-888-266-4226
For more information or to order direct visit **darkhorse.com** or call 1-800-862-0052 • Mon.-Sat. 9 A.M. to 5 P.M. Pacific Time
*Prices and availability subject to change without notice

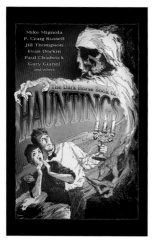

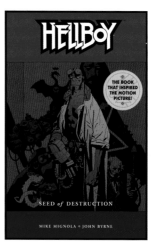

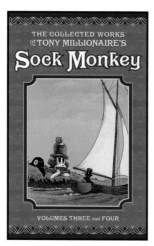

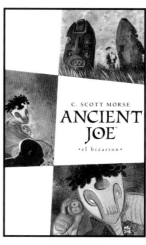

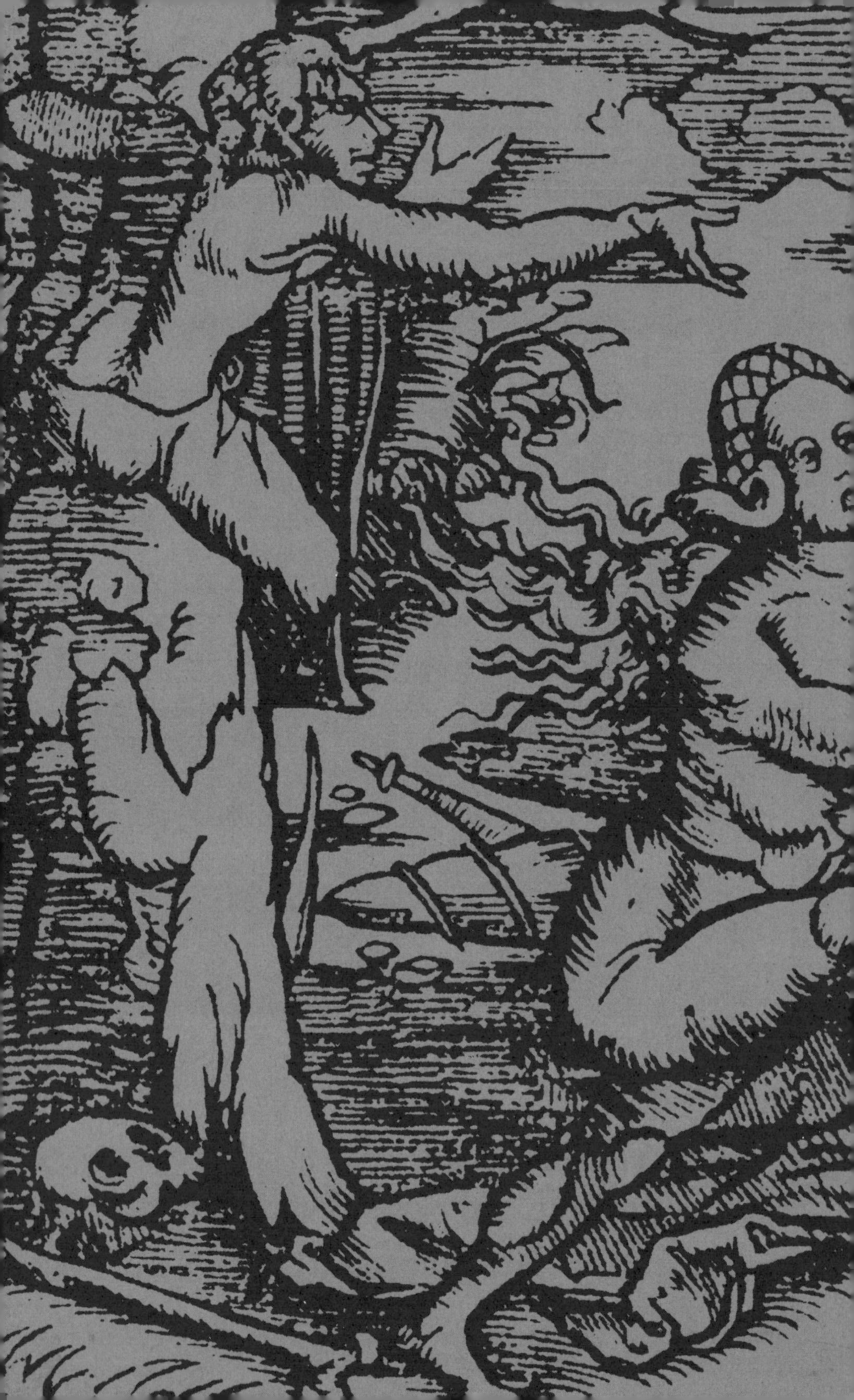